How to Be Fully Human

How to Be Fully Human

The Path to Freedom through Love

Paula Noronha Jordão, VDMF

Paulist Press
New York / Mahwah, NJ

Cover image by Keimani Storment / Shutterstock.com
Cover design by Sharyn Banks
Book design by Lynn Else

Original title: *Tan frágiles y tan amados. Una pedagogía para la libertad*, by Paula Jordão © Editorial Sal Terrae 2023 – Grupo de Comunicación Loyola, S. L. U. – Bilbao (Spain) gcloyola.com.

Library of Congress Cataloging-in-Publication Data
Names: Jordão, Paula Noronha author
Title: How to be fully human: the path to freedom through love / Paula Noronha Jordão.
Other titles: Tan fragiles y tan amados. English.
Description: New York : Paulist Press, [2025] | "Original title: Tan fragiles y tan amados. Una pedagogia para la libertad, by Paula Jordão © Editorial Sal Terrae 2023"- Grupo de Comunicación Loyola, S. L. U. – Bilbao (Spain) gcloyola.com. | Includes bibliographical references. | Summary: "This book is aimed at the broad Christian audience, especially those who seek to be faithful and to live in everyday life the freedom that God offers us: to be loved and to love"—Provided by publisher.
Identifiers: LCCN 2024051559 (print) | LCCN 2024051560 (ebook) | ISBN 9780809157372 paperback | ISBN 9780809189052 ebook
Subjects: LCSH: Love—Religious aspects—Christianity
Classification: LCC BV4639 .J66 2025 (print) | LCC BV4639 (ebook) | DDC 231/.6—dc23/eng/20250514
LC record available at https://lccn.loc.gov/2024051559
LC ebook record available at https://lccn.loc.gov/2024051560

ISBN 978-0-8091-5737-2 (paperback)
ISBN 978-0-8091-8905-2 (ebook)

Published by Paulist Press
997 Macarthur Boulevard
Mahwah, NJ 07430
www.paulistpress.com

Printed and bound in the
United States of America

Contents

CONTENTS

List of Illustrations

Foreword

The presence of Etty Hillesum accompanies me as I present Paula Jordão's luminous book, *How to Be Fully Human*. Wasn't it also the experience of this young Jewish woman to feel deeply embraced in her vulnerability? Since I came to know her diary, I have been struck by the way the experience of an increasingly liberated love matures within her, along with her passionate transformative process toward freedom and acceptance of herself and of life as it is. And now these words of hers come to me, in tune with the conviction that runs through the pages of this book: "It is not enough to preach about you, my God, to bring you to light in hearts. We must clear in others the path that leads to you; and to do that, we must be great knowers of the human soul" (*Diary*, September 17, 1942).

I was first Paula Jordão's teacher, and I enjoyed her presentations in class; now I have the privilege of cherishing our adult friendship. On occasion, we have commented on the pain of meeting people whose lives are out of balance or barely accepted, after many years of following Jesus. Lives that are poorly integrated or have hardly been able to mature: with fears, with low esteem, with much suffering on a personal and relational level....What have we lost along the way? Why has the good news of Jesus not had a positive impact on our bodies, on our wounded psychology, on our affections, and on the way we weave our relationships?

This book responds to these concerns and proposes an itinerary, a pedagogical path, that aims to help us channel the yearning for unification that dwells within us. We discover that to mature means to live ourselves in a fuller way, in a greater acceptance of who we are and of this fragility that grows with the passing of the years. More aware of our vulnerability, but at the same time more aware of the splendor of God's love within us, more capable of delving into its source and of drinking from its flow of joy for the life that is being illuminated within us, abundantly; shared.

The *parabola about affectivity* is the portico that leads us to commit to the proposed path. We discover what our resistances are to receiving this free love offered to us—in many cases our own unconscious defenses—and how to overcome them in order to feel the healing effects of this love within us—in our body, thoughts, feelings, and affections of Jesus—so that, in our relationship with him, we may experience a gentle transformation in the totality of our being: *Appreciating the richness of our corporeality. Seeking for God in our sensations. Discovering our own needs and sources of affection. Acknowledging our own self-rejection, learning to pray with our affectivity*....These are the suggestions that this book offers us.

In these times, when it is all too easy to be seduced (and dazzled) by so many offers of entertainment, especially virtual ones, that limit our capacity to be present to ourselves and to others, it is urgent that we follow this *pedagogy toward freedom* that allows us to be lucid artisans of our own lives. This roadmap, drawn upon a rich biblical basis, guides us to increase our capacity to receive and give love; and it also traces, in the Ignatian way, the *threats and dangers* we encounter on the path toward a more liberated and full life, more loving and delicate in its concreteness. Its success lies in offering us pedagogical tools that help us to collaborate, or at least not hinder, the patient and constant work of the Spirit in us and in history.

Another axis that lies at the heart of the author's concerns is her desire to proclaim the gospel plausibly to the men and women of our time in a way that touches their innermost wounds and hidden longings: "*God waits for and needs our reciprocal response. He can love us without our collaboration, but he cannot complete a friendship with us without our puzzle pieces*" (see "Friendship as Journey and Goal" in the Conclusion). We feel that God liberates our freedom as we receive love and allow it to flow ever more widely, as there is room for more faces, and as our daily bonds become more gratuitous and more healing.

Behind these pages, the author reveals her own experience of the God of Jesus who seduced her and of the path of freedom that has opened and continues to open before her, for it will always be ahead of her, like the Promised Land within. I am sure that a thoughtful reading of the book, reflected on one's own life, will be of great benefit and will hopefully lead one to say, as Etty Hillesum expressed in her *Diary* on December 12, 1941, at a time that for her was both terrible and full of grace: "*My God, I thank you for creating me as I am. I thank You that I feel such a vastness within me, for this vastness is nothing other than being filled with You. There is room for many things in my life....*"

Mariola López Villanueva, RSCJ

Acknowledgments

Thanks to all those people who loved me deeply in a modest, intense, and true way. Thanks to everyone who crossed the threshold of my life; I am who I am today because of you. Thanks also to all those people who also let themselves be loved by me. Thanks to all the things we have shared, given away, and cherished, and that have made me who I am today. Thanks, because from the abundance of my heart, my mouth speaks, and my hands write.

To all of them, I am eternally grateful.

Introduction

In our Christian life, we are often told that we must aspire to live as Jesus lived, but seldom or never are we shown *how* to do it. We are also reminded of what is wrong, but rarely are we given concrete suggestions of how we can change and let God be our artisan in the reality that we are and in which we live. Although it is fundamental, it is not enough to understand what it means to live a good life, nor is it even enough to want to live it. Thought and will are not the only driving forces of our existence; we must explore and evangelize the other aspects of our being.

Despite the abundance of very good books, articles, and works on spirituality in today's world, we still need pedagogical proposals that offer "hows" for a spiritual life rooted in the knowledge of oneself and the God revealed in Jesus. We need "hows" that help personal prayer, especially prayer with the Word, that provide insightful perspectives for spiritual accompaniment and enable us to follow paths of radical and authentic conversion. It is urgent to propose accessible avenues for most Christians who seek to be faithful. There is a need to propose didactics for freedom incarnated in our fragile humanity that can be strengthened and liberated by grace to live God's will in all things. The challenge cannot be postponed.

How to Be Fully Human: The Path to Freedom through Love is an interwoven search made from anthropological, psychological, biblical, and spiritual "hows" to learn and come to live the freedom in love that God offers us, in our concrete day-to-day life. This book aims to make known some of the most important spaces that constitute us, offer tools and proposals for a guided tour of our inner world. And, in there, to allow ourselves to be embraced and transformed by God until we reach the goal that God sets for us.

The first step of the journey is to enter the often-unknown landscape of our inner selves so that we can come to know ourselves better, without masks.

Secondly, we will go inside the pottery of God's experience to discover the immense love with which God made and continues to make us. God ceaselessly comes to meet us and embrace us—in our fragility—where we are at, just as we are, defying our resistances and our sinfulness. We can only know ourselves through the One who thought us into existence, created us, and knows us best. It is God who objectively says who we are. Only God's love identifies, finds, ratifies, and recreates us.

Finally, we will continue the journey toward freedom, providing more concrete "hows" to let ourselves be loved, liberated, and transformed until we live according to who we are: daughters and sons so fragile and so loved. People who abandon the slavery of all that prevents us from letting ourselves be loved and from loving as we are loved, of all that impedes us from doing what God tells us to do at every step.

So let us begin. It is Jesus himself who comes and walks beside us, asking us what we are talking about, explaining the Scriptures until our eyes are opened, our hearts burn, and we can follow him wherever he guides us (cf. Luke 24:13–33).

1

Self-Knowledge of the Inner World

One of the ways toward God is undoubtedly the knowledge of our inner and secret world, where we discover ourselves and where God also reveals himself. A hidden world where the Creator communicates face to face with those who are called friends (see Num 12:8; John 15:15). An inner world that is often unknown to us and which we feel threatened by because we fear its complex ambiguity beyond our control. At the same time, a fascinating world that constitutes us as a sounding board. Right there we hear the melody of our history, the echoes of the memory that permeates us, the impact of what surrounds us, the sensitivity that shapes us, and the personality that characterizes us; a world where our experience of love, relationships, and the experience of freedom come into play.

We will only overcome the risk of being alienated from ourselves by becoming acquainted with this evocative, colorful, and terrible universe that inhabits us. Only in this way will we gain familiarity with who we are—above all, with who we are according to God our creator; we will know the reason of our existence, and we will live and relate to one another in fullness.

We are reminded of that famous and pressing phrase from Greek wisdom: "Know yourself." This inscription carved at the entrance to the fourth-century-BC temple of Apollo at

Delphi seems to imply that an uninterrupted encounter with God requires us to engage with our inner self. As demanding as that is, it is at the same time extraordinary.

In Matthew and Luke's Gospels, we find Jesus's well-known sentence that speaks to us of the need to recognize ourselves in truth to be able to help others without hypocrisy: "Why do you see the speck in your neighbor's eye, but do not notice the log in your own eye? Or how can you say to your neighbor, 'Let me take the speck out of your eye,' while the log is in your own eye? You hypocrite, first take the log out of your own eye, and then you will see clearly to take the speck out of your neighbor's eye" (Matt 7:3–5; Luke 6:41–42).

The desert fathers also knew this earnest demand. They tell us that the way to God is inevitably through us. In their wisdom resonates the impossibility of knowing God without first learning to know ourselves. The road that leads to God passes fundamentally through our human clay, passions, and inner movements that we are to welcome and accept, and with which we must also struggle.

This itinerary entails humility. St. Benedict, mirroring the words of Jesus, describes that we ascend to God paradoxically by descending to our reality: "Those who humble themselves will be exalted" (Luke 14:11; 18:14). The desert fathers insisted on true humility as a *sine qua non* condition for entering the mysteries of God. Humility is the foundation and construction material of the spiritual building. Without it, we run the risk of manipulating God for our own interests, deceiving ourselves, and even worse, using others for our human vainglory. Only through the humble acknowledgment of our indigence will we allow God to be God.

St. Augustine confirms that we can only approach God by descending and entering our inner sanctuary, for "wheresoever you are, wherever you pray. He that hears is within.... He that hears you is not beyond you; you have not to travel far, nor to lift yourself up, so as to reach Him as it were with your hands. Rather, if you lift yourself up, you shall fall; if you humble yourself, He will draw near you."[1]

St. Teresa stresses that true prayer is only possible if it is accompanied by the self-knowledge that leads to humility, which is walking in the truth that God reveals to us. To be humble is to recognize that without God we are nothing. So important is self-knowledge that, in her writings, Teresa never gets tired of repeating it in various ways: "Self-knowledge is the bread with which all delicacies, however delicate they may be, are to be eaten on this path of contemplative prayer, and without this bread they could not be sustained."[2]

St. Ignatius of Loyola leads us along the same paths. His *Spiritual Exercises* are an itinerary to reach freedom to "know, love and serve"[3] the Creator, conquering oneself, removing all disordered affections "without determining oneself through any tendency that is disordered"[4] to freely seek and find the will of God. It is easy to see that to remove disordered affections, one must, of course, come to know them. The *Exercises* offer an itinerary and a methodology that necessarily encompass self-knowledge.

In *Gaudium et Spes* 3, the Second Vatican Council reminds us that the "whole and entire" person is to be considered. It refers to the human being as a unity between "body and soul, heart and conscience, mind and will." Therefore, we cannot leave anything out in this journey toward the gift of freedom that God wants to give us freely as a gift.

In fact, what separates us most from God is not our vices, our instincts, or even the mysterious transcendence of God. The greatest hindrance to entering the experience of the divine is the great ignorance of what goes on in our hearts. We know a lot about many things, but we are illiterate about our inner world, and this leads us to end up living in a way that is superficial and banal. Jesus himself invites us to visit our interior self: "But whenever you pray, go into your room and shut the door and pray to your Father who is in secret; and your Father who sees in secret will reward you" (Matt 6:6).

The life in abundance or holiness, to which we are all called, presupposes cultivating our soil, distinguishing hardness, stones, and thorns (cf. Matt 13:1–8). In this way, we will make room for the power of grace that makes the seeds planted by God in us germinate and grow, although we do not know how (cf. Mark 4:26–29).

The Affectivity Parabola

We will learn to immerse ourselves in our inmost being even when we are short of breath, in the certainty that, in all that we are, God loves us unconditionally and without measure (see Rom 8:31–38), embracing, probing, and knowing us (see Ps 139:1). To do this, we will follow a parabola (see Fig. 1), not a narrative in the style of the Gospel but a geometrical figure that evokes a well, an inward, downward path toward the deepest and most hidden side of us, and then upward again.

With each of its elements, this parabola is a result of my personal, spiritual, pastoral, and academic journey. It is the fruit of the inherited ecclesial wealth, of many authors, of what I have studied and received along the missionary journey, as well as of what I have learned through the accompaniment of many people and my own. It is also the fruit of my personal experience, the life of prayer, and the attempt to follow the ways of the gospel with many setbacks and achievements.

Fig. 1:
The Parabola

The affectivity parabola is the map to guide us through our interior. It will highlight some of the human realities that constitute us and that must be considered for self-knowledge from a Christian spiritual perspective. It does not, however, intend to cover all the complexity of our inner world, which cannot be defined or reduced to a single scheme.

Rather than an exhaustive explanation of each of these realities, "hows" will be given to help us go deeper and explore our inner world. It will always be possible to go further into each of the areas by studying their characteristics and interrelationships.

Later, we will explain why it is called "the affectivity parabola." In the discussion, we will discover that we are not only inhabited by thoughts and feelings but also by many other realities that "in-form," "con-form," and "shape" us—sensations, thoughts, feelings, needs, affectivity, desires, will, decisions, and actions (see Fig. 2). The order of their presentation and their place in the geometric figure is neither rigid nor static. It can change from person to person. As we go deeper and get closer to the bottom of the parabola, we detect more hidden realities, harder to know because they are more unconscious and involuntary, as indicated by the gray shaded area. Furthermore, the surface of the parabola corresponds to that which is more familiar to us. At the same time, none of these realities are self-contained, so they are often not easy to distinguish and separate.

Let us now begin this expedition toward the knowledge of our inner world.

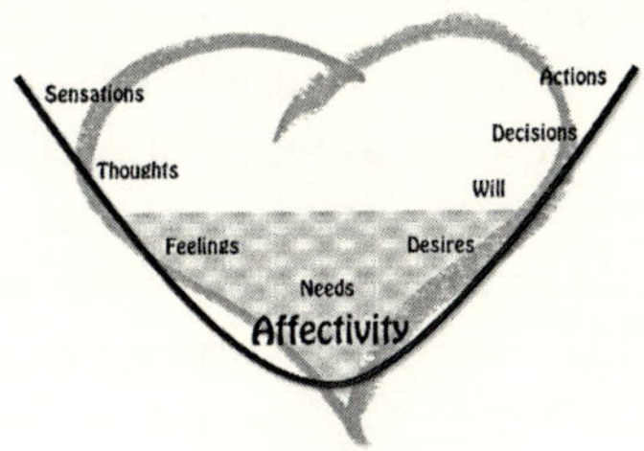

Fig. 2:
The Affectivity Parabola

Sensations

We are incarnated beings; we exist because we have a body that constitutes, conditions, determines, and gives us individuality. We can live neither ignoring our body nor working against it. We cannot separate the spiritual from the human, let alone the corporeal. We are one. Our faith begins with and believes in the incarnation of God in our human flesh. If we were to forget the relationship between body and spirit, nature and grace, heart and mind, interiority and exteriority, we would empty the content of the incarnation and deny God's way of being, of becoming man. Moreover, we would be denying ourselves. The body is often forgotten in books on spirituality, and yet it is the great gift God has given us as a possibility to be human. It is our treasure.

Therefore, the first reality we consider is our body with its sensations. Sensation is the experience produced in our body by the action of an external or internal trigger—light, sound, heat, sickness, relaxation, and so on—that is transmitted to the brain giving rise to perception. These stimuli—external and internal—are objective and, in contact with our body, produce subjective perceptions. For example, in a room at seventy-five degrees Fahrenheit (objective data), the perception for some people may be of cold, for others of warmth, and others of well-being (subjective data).

Knowing what inhabits us requires being attentive and perceptive to what our body lives and experiences. The body is the window—receiver and transmitter, channel and bridge—of the relationship with everything that surrounds us. The external world enters a relationship with our inner self through the body, and we manifest what we are inwardly also through the body. The body expresses and reveals our unique identity.

All our communication is bodily. And, according to some studies, at least 75 percent of our human communication is nonverbal. The body is always communicating through the gaze, face, tone of voice, words, silences, rhythms, gestures, posture, hand movements, head and body inclination, physical distance from others and things, how we dress, our external appearance, and so on. Without us noticing it, we receive all this communication through the door of our senses. It is through our senses that this wealth of information reaches our inner self; it is thanks to our senses that we grasp what is external to us.

Our body is a gateway into our interior that allows us to recognize not only how we relate to the external but also what impacts, affects, and inhabits us. It is essential to be attentive to what is happening in our body and perceive what is happening to it. Focusing on the sensations, we have given ourselves information about the world around us and the inner world that constitutes us, assimilates, reacts, and responds to so many stimuli.

We need to approach our sensations without judging them as bad or exalting them, in advance, as imperative or infallible. Deciphering our body signs implies welcoming them. Our body also manifests God's will to us as it hides and externalizes the treasure that we are. We must learn to value this pearl of great value received from God (cf. Matt 13:44–46).

We may confuse or overlap sensations and feelings that, although different, are interrelated and can even be referred to with the same words. Sensations, however, refer to the physical and perceptible manifestations that we can observe in ourselves or in others. Review the nonexhaustive "List of Sensations" in the appendix as an example. These words help us to increase our vocabulary and name our sensations as the first stop on this journey.

Thoughts

Thought is the human mental capacity to analyze, understand, and evaluate what is happening both inside and outside of us. It can be an idea, concept, image, memory, judgment, calculation, imagination, word, ideal, and much more. Thoughts are meanings and representations created by the mind to understand, reason, analyze, formulate, read, and relate to reality. It is a self-reflective capacity of inner and outer awareness. It is meta-knowledge by thinking about the thought itself.

Thoughts shape and form us. To know ourselves is to know what we think, what we understand, how we understand the world around us, and how we think about ourselves and others. It is also important to look at the values and ideals we proclaim, what we consider to be good or bad, and to understand what the norms are that rule us.

It is not easy to determine the limits of how we are dealing with thoughts or feelings. However, a major difference between the two is that thought is more rational and voluntary than feeling, more conscious and manageable.

The relationship and adherence to God and the kingdom entails our thinking as one of the human faculties par excellence. The image we have of God entirely conditions our way of relating to God and our way of living. It is vital to know what we think about God and to be aware of the rational content that brings us closer to or distances us from the gospel.

In this journey of inner knowledge, we often need to ask ourselves: "What do I think?"; "How do I think?"; and "Do I think?"

It is about becoming aware of the thoughts that inhabit us, perceiving whether we think for ourselves or let others think for us, whether we have our own thoughts or repeat what others say. It is also important to be aware of what we think inwardly about each situation and whether we act reflexively or impulsively.

The way we learn or don't learn new things also gives us clues about the way we think. Similarly, thinking relates to our creative capacity, so knowing our intellectual capacity includes pondering the following questions: Am I a creative person in my thinking, or do I try not to think "outside the box"? In new situations, do I apply the knowledge I already have, or do I run out of ideas, afraid to step out of my comfort zone?

Among the many questions that could be asked, there is one that is central to personal awareness: To which part of the inner world do I pay more attention—the emotional or the rational? Some people give more attention to the rational part, whereas others prefer to focus on the emotional part. This has consequences for our personality, on the decisions we make, and on how we live and relate to others.

Western culture has given much weight to thoughts. Reason has been exalted over the last century as capable of knowing, encompassing, conceiving, and explaining everything. The rational, the reasonable, the ideological, the scientific, and even the pseudoscientific have acquired much relevance in European and Western society even amid cultural diversities: we have come to doubt everything that is not scientifically verifiable, undervaluing other aspects of the inner world—equally real but not provable. Other continents and cultures value thoughts differently. In any case, it is not enough just to be attentive to thoughts. We must move on to another dimension of our interior, perhaps more difficult to know but very eloquent: our feelings.

Feelings

Further down the parabola, we come to feelings. Although these are an integral part of our very nature, we are illiterate in this area. We are versed in many areas, but our feelings often constitute the most mysterious black hole in our own universe.

The concept of feeling or emotion[5] is an inner tendency, energy, and movement that pushes us in a certain direction. It is either of attraction, to anything intuitively valued as good, or of rejection, if it is valued as bad. Feelings are therefore tendencies of action but, by themselves, are not responsible for our actions, as they are neither controllable nor voluntary, nor can they be judged morally.

We cannot provoke or change our feelings à la carte: I cannot tell myself how to feel—happy or anxious, for example—because our emotional world does not work like that. It should also be noted that feelings often go away soon after they appear, so we don't always have to keep track of them or pay too much attention to them. But if they remain, we need to attend to them.

Emotions are not always easy to live with, yet they have a strong influence on our motivation and behavior. I can decide to behave in one way or another, even conditioned by the feelings I experience; this means that my feelings are not the ones that decide and are not responsible for my actions. However, we are often inadvertently led by our emotions because they are unknown and even uncontrolled.

Let's look at some examples. I may "feel like or not feel like" talking to the people I live with when I get home, but I can still do what I think is good and right. I can be "more anxious" and yet not respond unkindly to another person. I can open the fridge and be "attracted" to a chocolate cake but don't necessarily have to eat it; I have the power to decide to do so or not, independently and beyond my feelings. I may be "lazy" to finish a task, but I can still try.

Usually, we label some feelings as bad or negative and others as good or positive, attributing moral value to them. We say that feelings are "bad or negative" when we don't like them, for they push us in the direction of what is not convenient for the situation in which we live, are not socially appropriate, or push us to do something morally reprehensible. We qualify as "good or positive" those feelings that are pleasurable, that we like, or that push us to act in a morally acceptable way. But there are no bad or good, negative or positive feelings; rather, we experience more pleasant and unpleasant feelings, feelings of satisfaction and dissatisfaction.

I may feel envious of someone because I see that they receive affection or have talents that I do not have and value as something desirable. Now, this is not necessarily a bad thing. Such envy can lead me to ask for help, to learn from that person or the talents he or she has. It would be wrong to treat that person badly, to invent manipulations to make him or her lose what he or she has, or to believe that I am greater or less than that person because I think that he or she is more loved than I am, or because he or she has more talents. This complex constellation of inner movements goes beyond the initial feeling, which, in itself, is not responsible for all the subsequent, reflexive, and voluntary development that can occur.

In English, there are more than three hundred terms to express feelings. In our emotional vocabulary, we barely use fifteen of them. To the question, "How do you feel?" we limit ourselves to answering, "I feel happy, sad, good, bad, tired, nervous, irritated, afraid, enthusiastic, bored, and not much more." Knowing our inner world involves increasing our emotional dictionary to be able to describe, inform, and feel ourselves. Review the non exhaustive "List of Feelings" in the appendix.

Needs

One step further inward meets our needs that, as the name suggests, are deficiencies that we experience. They are also potentialities or capacities that manifest themselves seeking fulfillment and therefore drive us to action. They are natural, for we are created incomplete, limited, capable, and needy, in the process of becoming. Although they are profoundly human, we tend to fear and mistrust them. We talk little about them and how to address them in the context of following Jesus without repressing or idolizing them—the other dangerous extreme. If, on the one hand, some try to deny their needs, others live at the mercy of what they need, being slaves to them to the point of enslaving others.

We find it very difficult to be in touch with our needs, from which we tend to distance ourselves almost completely. However, it is only by acknowledging them that we can live more realistically, more fully and happily. If we do not recognize them, we can become frustrated, fussy, demanding, and quarrelsome because we will lack what we need to live. A need is not a fleeting whim but rather something that we have to satisfy basically to achieve a healthy and balanced human life.

As with feelings, we also need the right terminology to know our needs, formulate them, and express them. In the appendix, you will find a list of needs that, without pretending to be exhaustive, will help in this process.

Needs are transversal to all areas of our existence and are not accessories. We can do without what we have, but we cannot do without who we are; we are beings with needs! Among these needs are some that are more physical and basic, others that are more social and relational, and those of human and spiritual fulfillment, the satisfaction of which points to the meaning of life.

Talking again about emotions, we emphasize that they are not the responsibility of others, as we often live, believe, and express: "I am unhappy because my mother..."; "I am angry because you..."; "I am frustrated because of my brother..."; "I am tired because of my boss..."; "I am devastated by the confusion that she...." But it is not so. We cannot hold others responsible for the feelings we have, nor can we take responsibility for the feelings that others may feel. Feelings originate from the needs we experience firsthand and from what we think, expect, and interpret when faced with the events we experience, and what others say and do.

Feelings are a consequence of our satisfied or unsatisfied needs in the great entanglement of what happens to us inside and outside. We can, therefore, define "feeling" as the symptom that indicates the satisfaction or dissatisfaction of our needs within us. If the needs are satisfied, the feelings are pleasant and agreeable; on the other hand, if the needs are not satisfied, the emotions are less agreeable and even unsettling.

Fear of needs can come from the strong emotions they provoke, from the strength of their emptiness that demands a response, or even from their satisfaction that makes us joyful but can often be disconcerting. This fear can also arise from thinking that having needs, paying attention to them, or talking about them is bad, unchristian, or selfish, preventing us from being attentive to the needs of others. However, this is a contradiction: How can I be aware of someone else's needs if I am not first aware of my own? We can only succeed in being attentive, aware, and understanding of the needs of others if we are attentive, conscious, and aware of our own needs. If we are not aware of what we really need, we run the risk of projecting our own needs onto others, making them responsible for our emotional world, and using them to satisfy us in an unconscious, instinctive, and self-centered way. Moreover, we will find it difficult to make good decisions, because we will depend on others' opinions—on what they think or want, on norms, on what is implicitly imposed; likewise, we will change with the changing winds and become prisoners of what supposedly promises us some satisfaction.

Even without satisfying it, the mere fact of identifying a need brings considerable relief. We will only be able to develop appropriate, coherent, and realistic strategies and ask for help in meeting our needs if we identify them correctly. As this act often fails, we begin to live empty, frustrated, and restless lives without knowing why. We often fall into the tendency to blame others for our unmet needs and demand that they guess and respond without formulating and expressing them.

The ultimate responsibility for our needs and how we fulfill them is ours, even if we need others. We can neither resign ourselves nor demand that other people meet our needs.

Affectivity

Affectivity is one of our needs. It is the need for love: the hunger and thirst to be loved and to love. It is our deepest, most central, and most radical need. It is the area where we experience our value as a person; it is the deepest source of existence. The human person, created in the image and likeness of God who is love (cf. Gen 1:26–27; 1 John 4:8, 16), was created by and for love, and only in love is he or she fulfilled.

Affectivity is like a barometer that tells us whether we are experiencing being loved or not, as our needs demand and as we would like to be loved. At the same time, it shows us whether the love we offer to others is accepted in a way that is convenient, satisfying, and relevant to them and us.

Our affectivity, as well as our other needs, translates and registers in us through our feelings. If our need for affectivity is being satisfied, our feelings are of pleasure or well-being; if, however, it is not being satisfied, our feelings are of sorrow or discomfort.

Affectivity[6] is not only a need but also a capacity. To love and to be loved is both a need and a potential of the human being. Our human fulfillment is at stake here. This is the constitutive anthropology of the Christian faith. Our happiness, our personal fulfillment, our being like Jesus, and our being children in the Son depend on the love received, experienced, and offered to others (see John 15:1; John 4:7–21). "If I have all faith...but do not have love, I am nothing" (1 Cor 13:2). In love, life is fulfilled (cf. Rom 13:8–10).

Whether we are aware of it or not, affectivity is what determines us. The experiences of love or lack of love that we have shape us and make us unique. Undeniably, the love especially experienced in childhood, shared and developed throughout life, is what shapes us. Affectivity—felt through our skin when we are born—grows over the years without ever giving us any respite. Naturally, with age, not only does the thirst to receive love increase, but the capacity to love and to give oneself also grows. The years, well-lived and integrated, increase the capacity for affection. "Affection,"[7] in this context of affectivity, means all the actions of giving or receiving love that move us, impact us, and therefore affect us internally, creating a kaleidoscope of inner movements.

To say that affectivity governs and guides us is to recognize that it determines the motivations underlying our thinking, feeling, speaking, and doing. Many expressions that we think, say, and hear are loaded affectively: "But they didn't tell me"; "You didn't take me into account! You have done things without telling me"; "If I am asked gently, it feels good, if I am told as an order, it feels bad"; "If I am made to feel important, things go one way and I am available. If I am not made to feel important, things go differently and I don't feel like doing anything"; "If I feel loved, I am able to love back. If I don't feel loved I find it harder to love"; "If you appreciate what I do for you, I am happy, but if you seem to ignore what I have done, I will think twice before doing it again."

What each of these phrases—reflections of simple, everyday experiences—highlights is not so much the action itself, but what the person experiences affectively, the value he or she attaches to them, and the love that is shared or not shared. In other words, what matters most—also in the more complex situations where the objective and moral goodness of actions is at stake—is how we experience the fulfillment of our need to be valued, appreciated, and recognized; how we feel loved through the way the situations and the behaviors of the people involved unfolded; and how our offer of love has been useful, relevant, and accepted.

It is easy to recognize that it is often not so much the cherished ideas or values that cause conflict and division in relationships, but what is experienced emotionally, the feelings that arise, the fears that are awakened, and the needs that are neglected.

What impresses us and what we sense inwardly is the experience of affective satisfaction or dissatisfaction. This is what shapes and determines both our interior and our subsequent reactions, decisions, and behavior. However, in everyday life, we rarely realize the extent to which we are influenced by affectivity: if our affective need is fulfilled, then we feel loved, useful, valued, important, content, and eager to love; but if our affective need is unfulfilled, then everything becomes more difficult because we feel empty, needy, agitated, and discontented.

Recognizing this reality in our lives is vital but not easy. There is a reason why it is called "affectivity," since "affect" and "affectivity" are interrelated words. "Affectivity" is that which, radically, most "affects" us in our being, in our esteem and value as persons. The experience of affectivity determines our relationships with family; in friendship, community, and work; with ourselves; with everything that surrounds us; and with God. We have an affective thermostat that regulates and drives us internally.

In the situations in which we live, we make many inner

inquiries, often unnoticed and hidden, that basically have to do with our affectivity: Who is the protagonist, who carries out their way of doing things, who decides, how do they decide, who is listened to, do they like me, do I like them, do I like it, don't I like it, do they listen to me, can I love them, how can I please them, how can I be useful, do they value me, do they respect my needs, did I do it well? These and many other questions come to mind.

There is a dialogue between Mafalda and Susanita in Quino's drawings that illustrates very well how affectivity is central to our day-to-day life:

> Mafalda, with a book in her hand, says to Susanita: "I found something special for you Susanita. Listen to it. Woe to those who only care about what people will say."
>
> To which Susanita replies, leaving Mafalda dumbfounded: "Of course, what matters is what they have said, who has said it, how they said it, when they said it, from whom they said it, and why they said it...."[8]

If we walk the path of our most relevant, enjoyable, and fundamental human relationships, we soon realize that they involve a reciprocal, meaningful, and empathetic sharing of affection. Reciprocity and friendship grow when the shared affection responds satisfactorily to the mutual needs of each person, and both accept the gift that each person is. On the contrary, the relationships that are most difficult for us are those where our needs, mainly affective ones, are not adequately responded to or respected, or those where we are not able to meet satisfactorily, for whatever reason, the needs of the other—explicit or implicit, demanded or kept silent.

The name of this "affectivity parabola" derives logically from all this, because this is the background, the center, the focal point, and the culmination of all our inner journeys. Only by recognizing the experience in us of our affectivity will we discover what happens to us, who we are, who we think and feel ourselves to be. Depending on how we live and perceive our affectivity is how we are and how we love. On the one hand, a conscious, healthy, robust, and integrated affectivity will lead us to be free to let ourselves love and to love others. On the other hand, only by letting ourselves be loved and truly loving will we become free and fulfilled.

For all these reasons, it is not surprising that the message of the Beatitudes that Jesus proclaimed on the mountain as Good News is so costly and against the tide: to love those who do not always love us and may even be our enemies, and to love those who do not respond satisfactorily to our needs (see Matt 5). Because only a fulfilled affectivity can love, let us not forget that it is Jesus who invites us to let ourselves be loved and to recognize his love in our lives as the cause, source, and model of our love: "I give you a new commandment, that you love one another. Just as I have loved you, you also should love one another. By this everyone will know that you are my disciples, if you have love for one another" (John 13:34–35).

Affectivity as the capacity and need to love and to be loved is the gravitational center of Jesus's teaching. Jesus communicated to us what was central to his life: "As the Father has loved me, so I have loved you; abide in my love. If you keep my commandments, you will abide in my love, just as I have kept my Father's commandments and abide in his love....I have called you friends, because I have made known to you everything that I have heard from my Father" (John 15:9–10, 15b). We can only love like Jesus if we accept his love and if we make our home in him.

Desires

After having touched on affectivity, we move back up the affectivity parabola and come to desires. These are the impulses, interests, or cravings that push us internally to action, to achieve the satisfaction of our needs.

Desire is the outcome of a constellation of innumerable inner movements: sensations experienced, thoughts that value something as good or bad, feelings of attraction or rejection, needs that demand to be satisfied, and affectivity that seeks fulfillment, among many others. The Latin root of "desire" is *desiderare*, which etymologically means "to verify the absence of the stars" and evokes the absence of something or someone one longs for. Desire leads to the elaboration of strategies to obtain the ends sought, intertwining and bordering on will. The relationship between will and desire will be discussed later.

Some simple examples of our daily desires can be: "If I feel hungry, I need food, I desire to eat"; "If I feel lonely, I need a relationship, I desire company"; "In the face of someone's suffering, I feel empathy, I need to be useful, I desire to help in some way"; "In the life of following Jesus, I know and feel loved, I need and want to love, I desire to follow him and love him in his ways, loving those he entrusts to me."

These few examples allow us to see how needs, feelings, and desires are interconnected. It is easy to confuse the desire with the need and the strategy to satisfy it, but we cannot do this. The need is the lack that is felt and triggers the desire. The strategy is one of the various ways in which I can act or not act to achieve the satisfaction of the desire, since it can be satisfied in countless ways, or it can even remain unsatisfied if it is convenient: I can be hungry (need) and desire to eat (desire), but there are many possibilities (strategies) that draw the what, how, when, and how much I am going to eat, and I can even decide not to eat.

Of course, in our daily lives, it is not always so easy to distinguish what lies beneath our motivations: what we desire and why. We need time to ponder and decipher our motivational world of desires—a reality that cuts across all human dimensions: physical, intellectual, spiritual, social, work, and play. They can also be sustained over time and function as a compass that insists on seeking meaning in life, in situations, and in relationships. Desire seeks fulfillment and can unite all our forces toward something or someone that is considered fundamental. Therefore, desire cannot be thought of only as something irrational, instinctive, blind, or uncontrolled; it is often the force that keeps our motivation on track.

This reality of our inner world is also unpopular in Christian spirituality. It seems that desires are always bad, so they are to be suspected and locked away. The only thing that is allowed without suspicion is to desire God as if other desires were all disordered or in danger of being disordered. We cannot escape the fact that we would end up totally lost if we gave free rein to desires, ending up as prisoners of their claims. However, it would also not be healthy to always regard them with suspicion and prejudice, trying to stifle them.

Desires are essential in motivation, although not all of them have the same strength and should be considered in the same way. While they can misguide us, not knowing them honestly would undoubtedly lead us to be surreptitiously manipulated and betrayed by them, even if we fight tooth and nail to disable or disregard them.

In our society today, we are very often led to believe that all our desires need to be satisfied as a path to happiness because we cannot disregard any need. This leads to permanent instability and saturation and can even lead to a loss of the capacity to desire.

Although desire is strong and must be listened to, it need not be responsible for our actions. Nor does desire tell the whole truth about us, even if it has a strong influence, for we are not only what we desire. Therefore, our behavior in the face of desire needs to be prudent, considered, discerning, and magnanimous. Only with a great soul that makes us realistic, fearless, and creative people will we be able to respond appropriately to our desires, without stinginess and indulgence.

We can and must recognize our desires, indicators of our deepest thirst, even when we find it difficult. Although the word "thirst" indicates a physical lack, we use it as a synonym for longing, as it is also found in the biblical language (see Isa 55:1–3; John 4; John 7:37; Matt 5:6).

The deep desire is a throbbing yearning that needs to be attended to because it will not cease to disturb us. Whatever it is, desire uncovers us, reveals us, motivates us, and does not leave us in peace. Our desires speak of what we carry inside us, of the desired direction, of the sought goal in our pilgrimage toward the meaning of existence; they also testify to what we lack. Desires shape us, because they are the emptiness inhabiting us and aspiring to the fullness of love; they are our polar star, they indicate the coordinates that position us on the map of life, specifying our north; they are the wind that blows in our sails with impatience to arrive; they are the eagerness that invades us from "the spring that flows and runs, although it is night."[9]

Will

After the desires, we continue up the parable and meet the will, which is the capacity to want, to take a certain disposition about what we experience. It is the capacity for self-determination in the face of the diversity of inner movements and external demands.

The will is essential to existence. Without it we would live at the mercy of our instincts and emotions without a consolidated direction to guide us. Our will enables us to remain faithful to our commitments even when our feelings, desires, or needs push us in a different direction. A lack of willpower or a weak will that moves only to the rhythm of the most voluble inner motions harms the person and those around them because of their behavior's lightness, instability, and unpredictability. It is necessary to have the willpower to be responsible, free, and committed people who seek the good amid and despite everything.

However, we can fall into the fallacy of believing that it is enough to will for our inner world, and for our behaviors to obey our will. Even if we were strong-willed, our motivations, reactions, and decisions would not always respond to the commands of our will. Moreover, a rigid will can be harmful because it does not allow room for natural movements, human processes, life rhythms, necessary balances, or listening to all the elements that inhabit us. Pope Francis warns us not to fall into a conception in which we believe and affirm that everything can be achieved by willpower. That would be a Pelagian or semi-Pelagian mentality that may even speak of God's grace but deep down relies only on human capacity, as if willpower could substitute God's action in our lives.[10]

"What do you want?" Asking and answering this question leads us to become aware of what we really want as a basis for our decisions and actions. Sometimes we may say we will do something, but deep down we don't really want to do it, and that can create a lot of inner division. The reality is that if we don't want to do it, we won't do it (see Matt 21:28–32), or if we do it, we do it reluctantly, with negative consequences for ourselves and even possible retaliation toward others.

If we know that we don't want to do it, we can also choose to do it for other stronger reasons. Then we can formulate that

"I want to do what I don't really want to do," and, therefore, I am free to do it. This is what Jesus and many saints in history experienced. They went against their will because they wanted to do God's will lovingly by seeking the good of others above their own: "Sacrifice and offering you do not desire, but you have given me an open ear. Burnt offering and sin offering you have not required. Then I said, 'Here I am; in the scroll of the book it is written of me. I delight to do your will, O my God; your law is within my heart'" (Ps 40:6–8; cf. Rom 12:1–2).

We need to notice what moves our will. Good ideas or values have a strong motivational force, but they do not always move us by themselves. Rationality is not always enough to convince the will. Our emotional world and affectivity also have a decisive influence on what we want. While we must recognize the real affective weight that the values and ideals we profess have on us, we cannot naively ignore that many times these values and ideals encounter substantial emotional resistance within us, conditioning, slowing down, blocking, and even diverting our will. Holiness leads us along paths of integration where we can affirm with the psalmist: "My heart and my flesh sing for joy to the living God" (Ps 84:2).

Several questions help us to get to know ourselves better: What is the weight of willpower in our lives? Do we have the willpower, or are we more at the mercy of situations, others, or feelings? In any situation, what do we want, and what do we not want? What emotional value—what resistances and attractions—do we experience when faced with the values and ideals we claim to want in life (e.g., prayer, generosity, sacrifice, community...)? In the relationships we live, do we listen to the will of others, do we yield, or are we more inclined to seek to do our own will?

And what is the relationship between desire and will?

Desire, on the one hand, is more connected to emotions, to the sometimes-unrealistic aspiration for the satisfaction of needs, dreams, and fantasies that we may have. Will, on the other hand, is—or needs to be—more connected to thought, to the values we profess, to human limits, and to the realism that life imposes on us.

Desire brings energy, color, and enthusiasm. Will means reality, determination, and maturity. Balance occurs when there is a dance between these two dimensions, where will protects the person from uncontrolled desire. Desire, nevertheless, safeguards the vital breath.

This does not mean that desire and will must always be opposed to each other or that there must be a constant titanic struggle between them. Rather, there needs to be a constant dialogue between them, a search for what is good and what is right—that is, discernment. Neither can the will impose itself severely nor desire be the tyrant with its whims. It is therefore necessary to articulate desire and will in the realm of decision-making. If both are well intertwined, they bring a positive dynamism to life.

Decisions

In life, beyond simply having the will, it is necessary to decide and to make up one's mind. A decision is the active and practical choice of a determined behavior, attitude, or response to a concrete situation. Faced with a particular scenario, the person decides to do something specific.

Sometimes it is not easy to decide, but not deciding is already a decision. The more options one has, the more difficult the decision becomes, because to choose one thing is necessarily to renounce another; however, only by deciding can one move forward. To choose is to open a door even if others are closed.

The decision-making sphere is easier to comprehend. Additionally, understanding the decisions we make enables us to continue to know ourselves. On the threshold of decisions, there are many possibilities: I can want and never decide to do what I want; I can want one thing and decide to do another; I can have no power to decide to do what I want; I can decide and do what I want.

Decisions are many in life, and we spend our time, from when we get up in the morning until we get up again the next day, making decisions. We are bound to have to decide. Decisions are part of the simplest and most complex parts of our lives.

Not all decisions have the same weight and importance. Some mark a fundamental direction in life (the choice of life status, career, the person you decide to live with, whether or not to have children), and others change daily (what you decide to eat, which way to go to work, the clothes you wear, and so on). The most important decisions are those that most define us, have the greatest consequences for the future, and make us who we are, so they require the most thought and commitment on our part. Yet the simplest decisions also require consistency and coherence with our most important decisions and fundamental life choice.

To know our decisions, we need to look at the life we lead and ask ourselves: What decisions have I made, why, what consequences will these decisions have or have they had in practice?

When making decisions, it is also important to look at the inner difficulties or ease we find in doing so. Some people put off indefinitely the big and small decisions that need to be made. Others are so afraid of making mistakes by deciding wrongly that they prefer not to decide at all. However, risk is part of life, and it is better to decide even when making mistakes than never to decide at all and make the serious mistake of indecision.

Other people, however, are very resolute, making decisions without due consideration. Recognizing this tendency fosters self-awareness both regarding decisions we have made in the past and those we make in the present in view of the future.

Before moving on to the next aspect of our interior, I leave the testimony of Viktor Frankl, who reminds us that the power to decide about our own attitude is always in our hands:

> The experiences of camp life show that man does have a choice of action. There were enough examples, often of a heroic nature, which proved that apathy could be overcome, irritability suppressed. Man *can* preserve a vestige of spiritual freedom, of independence of mind, even in such terrible conditions of psychic and physical stress.
>
> We who lived in concentration camps can remember the men who walked through the huts comforting others, giving away their last piece of bread. They may have been few in number, but they offer sufficient proof that everything can be taken from man but one thing: the last of the human freedoms—to choose one's attitude in any given set of circumstances, to choose one's own way.[11]

Actions

An action is the specific activity or behavior that a person performs. The decision needs to give rise to the action.

We are who we are, and we build ourselves through what we do, our behavior reflects our inner world. Therefore, it is necessary to be attentive to what we do or do not do, to what we say or do not say. All of this shows who we are, what constitutes us, and who we are becoming.

As popular wisdom states, "Hell is paved with good intentions." Knowing our behaviors leads us to discover the inner world that motivates them. Sometimes, we may have certain intentions, but our behavior seems to go in a different direction and may even contradict what we wanted to have said, done, and decided. This would indicate that there are other influences, perhaps beyond our control, that are conditioning us from within.

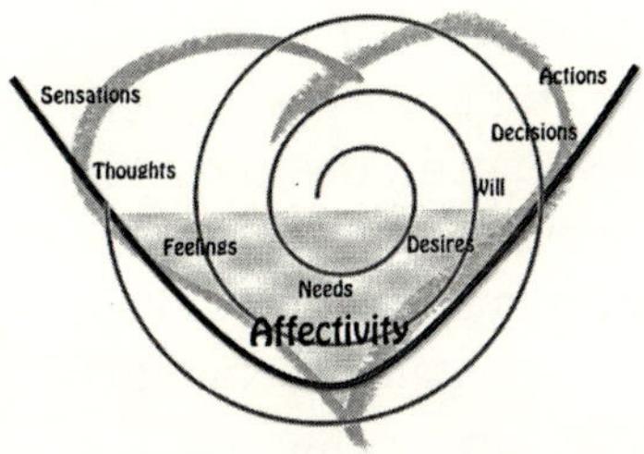

Fig. 3
Moving Forward in a Spiral

When we reach the end of this parabolic path, we need to start again. Our actions, carried out through our body, take us back to the initial step of our sensations, and so on, through our entire inner world. We are not always in the same place going around in circles, but we will advance in a spiral: we retrace the same inner spaces, but because we are no longer the same people as when we started, we will see new realities. We will discover different landscapes. We will learn to know ourselves better. We will grow in depth, leaving appearance on the surface. We will go deeper into our inner self that will become more familiar and at the same time always new.

Thus, we come to the end of the explanation of the affectivity parabola. However, two points are still essential to complete what has been said so far: the influence of the unconscious and psychological difficulties.

Two Essential Points

The Influence of the Unconscious

Amid all that has been presented, we cannot forget the presence of the unconscious in us. Exploring who we are will lead us to perceive that there are spaces and motivations within us that condition us but are difficult to recognize; sometimes we need specialized help to achieve this goal.

Usually, the unconscious is seen as something only bad or always problematic. However, even if it contains conflicting or traumatic contents, it also contains much positive, creative, and spontaneous emotional energy that brings color and enthusiasm to life.

Neither is the influence of the unconscious always decisive, nor is it all pathological, as sometimes may have been believed. There are various levels of influence of the unconscious, and it marks people in different ways without this always having to be considered as illness. We must accept the active presence of the unconscious, with its emotional factors, in normal people who are neither sick nor hopelessly sinful.

The influence of the unconscious can be seen in our inner processes, in prayer, and in our relationship with ourselves and with others, because it affects our sensations, thoughts, feelings, needs, affectivity, desires, will, decisions, and actions.

The best way to become aware of the influence of the unconscious is to be attentive to our inner world, especially to our feelings and the way we handle them.

Attempting to make conscious what is unconscious to us will make it possible to channel much energy within ourselves and allow us to know, purify, and release our most hidden motivations in truth and freedom toward God with the help of divine grace.

Psychological Difficulties

Some people also experience serious, even severe, psychological difficulties. Some of these problems can become pathological, leading to a loss of contact with reality or a loss of control over rationality, the emotional world, the will, the capacity for freedom, or our behavior.

In the same way, there are also present and past experiences that are traumatic and affect the inner world, leaving their mark in each of the areas presented, sometimes in a punctual way and sometimes in a chronic way. These experiences—such as illness, abuse (sexual, physical, psychological, or emotional), abandonment, major losses, accidents, among others—can become psychological difficulties that require special attention and often specialized professional help so that the person can discover, manage, and integrate their inner world.

End of the Tour

For the moment, our guided tour of our inner world is complete, but we will return to it later. With all that we have seen, we have discovered many places that we need to visit frequently if we want to embark on an adventure of self-knowledge.

It is not always easy to distinguish between the different areas of our interior that were mentioned above, but neither are we expected to make a microscopic observation of what is happening to us in order to obtain a static and inert x-ray. Rather, we seek to know what happens to us broadly and vitally, embracing the multiform variety of our movements and inner spaces. Consequently, we will discover ourselves inhabited by diverse dynamisms, we will get to know their manifestations, and we will glimpse how they are related to one another.

Training ourselves in this knowledge is an inevitable, humble, and arduous apprenticeship that requires dedication and accompaniment. This exercise is essential because becoming aware of what we shelter inside gives us invaluable intuitions and reconnects us with ourselves, calms us and frees us from within, and allows us to take possession of our interior and our responses without having to react ignorantly or impulsively. Learning and apprehending ourselves leads us to live as we really are, on pilgrimage toward what we are called to be.

However, we cannot walk this path alone, nor would it be convenient to do so. Knowing ourselves, usefully, truly, and healthily, is only possible from the loving perspective of God, who created us and continues to recreate us. In the next chapter, we raise our gaze to meet God's gaze.

2

We Are So Loved, Yet We Resist

Only God truly tells us who we are. Our most genuine identity is being unconditionally beloved children. Yet, this reality is mysteriously tough for us to believe, internalize, and live, and it is impossible to attain by our own efforts. We can only do it with the help of the grace that enlightens, justifies, and liberates us.

Through an anthropological, biblical, and theological approach, we will explore the reality of God's love offered to us—but which we resist— to explore the way forward. The chapter begins with the reality of God's eternal and unconditional love, manifested in Jesus, and then explains the resistances that trap us and prevent us from letting ourselves be loved just like that. It will end with Jesus's experience of the temptations that he had to face. This will teach us how to live our filial identity when confronted with the temptations that haunt us.

We Are Unconditionally Loved

We know, hear, and often repeat that God's love is totally gratuitous, unceasingly poured out, and patiently compassionate. In fact, in practical terms, we find it difficult to believe and even more difficult to live it. It is not easy for us to let ourselves be loved undeservedly and even unjustly, in our opinion, at every step and in every corner of our being. We believe, even if we do not make it explicit, that we must behave well to merit or earn love, justification, and salvation. These become a result of our efforts, our abilities, and moral perfectionism. However, God is far from being like this or treating us, as we often believe, how we deserve or do not deserve to be treated.

Fortunately, the saints have preceded us on the way. Teresa of Avila, for example, testifies that it was amid her crimes that she was most aware of God's undeserved love:

> O Lord of my soul! How can I ever pay tribute to the mercy you bestowed on me during those years? How could I ever express my gratitude for the moments when I turned against you and you swiftly brought me back, through the most extraordinary repentance, to taste your sublime gifts? Truly, my King, you chose the most delicate and painful punishment I could possibly have endured. You knew exactly what would break my heart open; you chastised my faults with great favors.[1]

Thérèse of Lisieux, in her turn, encourages us not to be afraid to always return to the love of God, even with wounded, empty, and dirty hands: "Even though I had on my conscience all the sins that can be committed, I would go, my heart broken with sorrow, and throw myself into Jesus' arms, for I know how much He loves the prodigal child who returns to Him."[2]

We should never doubt or hide from God's love because grace is immovable and everlasting. God's love is first and never second: "because he first loved us" (1 John 4:19). As Pope Francis tells us, God's love *first took the initiative* (see *Evangelii Gaudium*, 24).

There is nothing we can do that will move God to love us less, just as there is nothing that will move God to love us more. God's love for each person will never pass away or change:

> For the mountains may depart
>   and the hills be removed,
> but my steadfast love shall not depart from you,
>   and my covenant of peace shall not be removed,
>   says the LORD, who has compassion on you.
>   (Isa 54:10)

God loves us with an eternal love (cf. Jer 31:3), and nothing can change that. Moreover, God comes to look for us in our mistaken ways and is overjoyed when we allow ourselves to be found (cf. Luke 15).

It is in Jesus that God became known to us in a sublime and unexpected way, which is why we need to fix our gaze on him, the visible expression of the invisible God (cf. John 1:18; Col 1:15).

Let us go down with him to the river Jordan where he allows himself to be baptized by John the Baptist. This experience of Jesus draws us into his identity. When God speaks at the baptism of Jesus, he does not speak only of himself but also of who the Son is. God does not say: "I love you" but rather: "This is my Son, the Beloved, with whom I am well pleased" (see Matt 3:17; Luke 3:22). God reveals not only who the Father is but also himself by drawing back the veil on who Jesus is. The Father's intervention at the river Jordan seems to answer the question, "Who is this?" The answer is clear: "This is my beloved Son." Jesus, for his part, is the one who believed and lived his whole existence being profoundly who he was, supported by this immovable love of God that made him be, therefore, giving him his real identity (cf. John 10:17; 17:23, 26).

But the love that Jesus experienced was not only for his own sake. Jesus himself tells us: "As the Father has loved me, so have I loved you. Now remain in my love" (John 15:9). All the love that Jesus received and experienced from the Father, all the outpouring of love is also, and essentially, for us; it is destined to be ours through the filiation that is freely and generously offered to us. That is what we were created for: "He chose us in Christ before the foundation of the world to be holy and blameless before him in love. He destined us for adoption as his children through Jesus Christ, according to the good pleasure of his will" (Eph 1:4–5).

Each one of us is also God's beloved child. God's words at the Jordan River are offered to every human being, regardless of religion or belief:

> See what love the Father has given us, that we should be called children of God; and that is what we are. The reason the world does not know us is that it did not know him. Beloved, we are God's children now; what we will be has not yet been revealed. What we do know is this: when he is revealed, we will be like him, for we will see him as he is." (1 John 3:1–2)

The great purpose of the Son's incarnation is to enable our knowledge of God's love for us, to believe and live in him: "For God so loved the world that he gave his only Son, so that everyone who believes in him may not perish but may have eternal life. Indeed, God did not send the Son into the world to condemn the world, but in order that the world might be saved through him" (John 3:16–17; cf. 1 John 4:16). The incarnation and salvation intend that we become who we really are in Jesus, with him and like him: the beloved children in whom God is well pleased. Jesus, in his prayer to the Father, formulates the desire that guided his life: "(Father) that the world may know that you have sent me and have loved them even as you have loved me" (John 17:23).

His Spirit has been sent to make this reality possible in us by grace: "Because you are children, God has sent the Spirit of his Son into our hearts, crying, 'Abba! Father!' So you are no longer a slave but a child, and if a child then also an heir, through God" (Gal 4:6–7).

Each of Jesus's meetings narrated in the Gospels sought to touch each person through the ineffable love of God in his life: "Therefore, I tell you, her sins, which were many, have been forgiven; hence she has shown great love. But the one to whom little is forgiven, loves little" (Luke 7:47). We could gather here so many words and gestures of Jesus that confirm this reality.

At the same time, every disagreement he had with those who opposed him in the name of the law had no other purpose than to show them that God was different from what they thought: "Go and learn what this means, 'I desire mercy, not sacrifice.' For I have come to call not the righteous but sinners" (Matt 9:13). There are too many other examples like this to list here.

Through Jesus, the law and the prophets take on a new and immense depth. In him, we can recall God's love and grace already expressed in the Old Testament. Whatever happens, we will never cease to be God's image and precious in his sight (cf. Gen 1:31; Isa 43:5). God continues to love us and to keep us in existence, not out of a false paternalistic condescension that resigns itself to human wickedness and desertion but out of true love for what God created, creates, and continues to recreate:

> For you love all things that exist,
> and detest none of the things that you have made,
> for you would not have made anything if you had hated it.

How would anything have endured if you had not
 willed it?
Or how would anything not called forth by you have
 been preserved?
You spare all things, for they are yours,
O Lord, you who love the living. (Wis 11:24–26)

God loves us, as the friend who loves life, our life. The great proof is that God has created us. Had God not loved us, we would not have been given existence, nor would we have been kept in existence. God loves us as we are and not as we would like to be or even as we think we should be to please God or others. God also loves us in our sin, in our mud, and never despite it:

The Lord is merciful and gracious,
 slow to anger and abounding in steadfast love.
He will not always accuse,
 nor will he keep his anger forever.
He does not deal with us according to our sins,
 nor repay us according to our iniquities.
For as the heavens are high above the earth,
 so great is his steadfast love toward those who fear
 him;
as far as the east is from the west,
 so far he removes our transgressions from us.
As a father has compassion for his children,
 so the Lord has compassion for those who fear him.
For he knows how we were made;
 he remembers that we are dust. (Ps 103:8–14)

All that has been said so far is not new, we know it and we often formulate it in our faith, but it is very difficult for us to let it become flesh of our flesh, air of our lungs, physiognomy of our deepest contours, and source of our life. That is why it is essential to listen to it and repeat it, to breathe it in and savor it, to read it and ask for this reality until it becomes our own. We remember here the author of Deuteronomy, who asked his people in the name of God:

> Keep these words that I am commanding you today in your heart. Recite them to your children and talk about them when you are at home and when you are away, when you lie down and when you rise. Bind them as a sign on your hand, fix them as an emblem on your forehead, and write them on the doorposts of your house and on your gates. (Deut 6:6–9)

And what words did God give them? We dare to take a leap and let Jesus, once again, answer the words of the Old Testament recorded in the New Testament:

> "You shall love the Lord your God with all your heart, and with all your soul, and with all your mind." This is the greatest and first commandment. And a second is like it: "You shall love your neighbor as yourself." On these two commandments hang all the law and the prophets. (Matt 22:37–40; cf. Deut 6:5; Lev 19:18)

At another point Jesus adds: "This is my commandment, that you love one another as I have loved you" (John 15:12). The "*as*" not only signifies a model of love—love one another *as* I love—but it is also and above all the cause of our love: love one another because I have loved each one of you.

We can only love in the present and future because, in the past, present, and future, we were, are, and will be very loved. Whatever happens, we are loved, cared for, and given grace. This will never change on God's part, who always and in everything works for our good (cf. Rom 8:28). Fortunately, this is the great good news that Jesus came to give us. Good news written not with ink but with his flesh and blood, ratified on the cross, corroborated by his unexpected resurrection, and by the outpouring of his Holy Spirit in our hearts (cf. Rom 5:5).

The apostle Paul, from his experience of God's love, challenges and questions us with his many questions: "What then are we to say about these things? If God is for us, who is against us?...Who will separate us from the love of Christ?" (Rom 8:31–35). Paul will answer them with the experienced certainty that nothing and no one can separate us from the love of God manifested in Christ Jesus, neither our sin nor our deepest resistances, nor our past mistakes, nor the evil that others have done to us, nor our doubts with an emotional appearance of truthfulness, nor our noncompliance or legalistic fulfillment of the law. His love in us makes us conquerors (which presupposes a struggle on our part) over all that threatens to separate us from God and the saving dynamic in us. For in him, we have the unshakeable conviction that the Son of God "loved me and gave himself for me" (Gal 2:20).

Furthermore, God's grace in us is made perfect in weakness (cf. 2 Cor 12:9–10). If this is so, we must allow God to enter into us or ask to enter into God, amid our frailty and even in the abundance of our sin, until the cascade of God's love floods over us and grace abounds mightily in us (cf. Rom 5:20).

We need to heal the image or idea we have of God and the idea we think God has of us. We need to let God, again and again, reconfigure us into who we are—the image and likeness of God (cf. Gen 1:26; Jer 18:1–5)—and we need to rediscover the true face of God (cf. John 1:18; Pss 27; 31).

We Resist Letting Ourselves Be Loved

We all carry within us a force that breaks us, contradicts us and distances us from God. In the face of God's unceasing love, we need to discover the impetus that leads us to resist so much love and to doubt God. This inner reality distorts the face of God, what he is saying to us, and what he is asking of us, leading us by the reins of our lives into paths of lies. It is essential to recognize that we are indeed loved unconditionally but that we existentially rebel and run away from that love. Let us now turn our attention to this human condition.

Our limited human condition prevents us from knowing God as God is, leading us to try to manipulate, control, and define God in our own way. Our sin (which entails the denial of God, of his unconditional love, and of who we are before him) needs to be unmasked if we are to allow God to liberate us from within through love. We cannot underestimate how difficult it is to believe in the true God as Jesus teaches us, in his incarnation, in his way of living, dying, and rising again. We can only achieve this with his grace, with much truth and inner conversion (cf. Mark 10:27, 51; John 15:5).

The opening pages of Genesis alert us to the fact that, existentially engraved in each of us, there is a hard uncertainty, a disturbing doubt, a powerful temptation made up of fear and shame. We doubt God's gratuitous love in our naked vulnerability: Will God always love us? Does God always want our good? Does God always forgive us despite everything? Does God bet on us? Will God care for us? Will God come to meet our needs? Will God make his face shine upon us? Will God invest in our future, as small as we are, and with all the good and bad that we do?

The fear that we are not good enough and not worthy of being loved for who we are threatens us. Even if we are not always aware of it, the feeling of unworthiness pervades and determines us. This suspicion, so inspiringly expressed at the beginning of the Bible, is the great tragedy we humans share with Adam and Eve. And so, both they and we live the tragedy of disobedience because we doubt God. Let us consider this further.

God created Adam and Eve full of beauty, created them very well: "God said, 'Let us make humankind in our image, according to our likeness; and let them have dominion over the fish of the sea, and over the birds of the air, and over the cattle, and over all the wild animals of the earth, and over every creeping thing that creeps upon the earth.' So God created humankind in his image, in the image of God he created them; male and female he created them" (Gen 1:26–27). "God saw everything that he had made, and indeed, it was very good. And there was evening and there was morning, the sixth day" (Gen 1:31).

Then God told them not to eat of the fruit of the tree of the knowledge of good and evil: "And the LORD God commanded the man, 'You may freely eat of every tree of the garden; but of the tree of the knowledge of good and evil you shall not eat, for in the day that you eat of it you shall die'" (Gen 2:16–17).

But we already know that they disobeyed and ate. What happened? The serpent tells them that they can eat because what God claims is not true, but that God fears human rivals: "But the serpent said to the woman, 'You will not die; for God knows that when you eat of it your eyes will be opened, and you will be like God, knowing good and evil'" (Gen 3:4b–5). Faced with this, they doubt God's goodness, they doubt their own identity, and they forget that they were already like God, made in God's image and likeness.

By disobeying God, Adam and Eve try to snatch for themselves what has already been freely offered to them, without having to earn it through effort. But they go even further. The disobedience, which was already serious, became enormously disproportionate when the human couple, having done the wrong thing, hid from God. They listen to God in the garden, but when they realize that they are naked, they are ashamed, terrified that they will be seen as they are, barely covered with fig leaves; they run away from God, hiding among the trees of the garden (see Gen 3:7–11).

Before eating the fruit of the tree, "the man and his wife were both naked, and were not ashamed" (Gen 2:25). Before, they knew, believed, and lived that they were full of beauty, full of goodness, very good, like God. But afterward, they were ashamed; we are ashamed. They hide; we hide. They are afraid; we are afraid. They flee; we run because we are afraid. We are afraid because we are ashamed of not being good enough to be loved in our fragile, seemingly shameful, overly vulnerable nakedness (cf. Gen 2:25). The temptation of falsehood and ugliness is stronger. The result is that we insist on hiding from ourselves, from others, and from God, avoiding simply being who we are in our vulnerability, and we fall into the trap of rejecting ourselves. Consequently, we run away from who we are. We reject our *true self*; we reject ourselves; we deceive ourselves. We believe in a lie.

It is hard but it is real. We carry within us this tempting deception, this false belief—because it is a lie—that leads us to deny our true identity and makes us want to be who we are not in the illusion of making ourselves more worthy to be loved. We cover ourselves with fig leaves to disguise our nakedness and appear more beautiful. We deny and distrust who we really are and who others are. And then we cover ourselves and others with masks that seem to be our defense and protection, already since time immemorial and not just from viruses! Our pandemic is even more serious and has many variants that come from the same lineage: we need to disguise our human misery with whatever it is because who we are is not good and is no longer good in our eyes. Deep down, what inhabits and deceives us is the belief that we are ugly, that we are worthless, and that we are insufficient. We believe that we are ridiculous, that we are not nice, that we are small, and that we must prove the opposite in countless ways. Thus, we embark on the constant anxiety to prove our worth to ourselves and others by creating an alternative identity: *a false self.*

We are like gods (cf. Psalm 82:6; John 10:34). We are as loved as Jesus was, but we do not believe it. We doubt, suspect, falter, and are overcome by the great seduction of lies. We fall into the great temptation of doubting our most fundamental truth and end up living in alienation.

When we look at our history, we can discover many people who have loved us deeply and well, allowing us to discover the best of ourselves. But at the same time, these same people, or others, as well as so many events in our lives, have caused us to doubt the beauty that we are because they have mistreated us and even hurt us, dislocated us, and led us to be convinced that we are not worthy or adequate. Faced with our genetic, familial, and historical baggage, we either affirm the goodness and beauty that constitute us or deny it, confirming and deepening our existential doubt, our self-rejection. How many traumas, blockages, wounds, and harsh experiences have been transformed by our perception into a lesser, fearful, and anxious identity, convincing us that we are diminished, unworthy, and unlovable?

Like Adam and Eve, we hide, we protect ourselves out of fear and shame. Like the servant in the parable who had a talent, we devalue ourselves, we project onto others the harshness of what we feel, and we bury our talents in fear: "Then the one who had received the one talent also came forward, saying, 'Master, I knew that you were a harsh man, reaping where you did not sow, and gathering where you did not scatter seed;

so I was afraid, and I went and hid your talent in the ground. Here you have what is yours'" (Matt 25:24b–25; cf. Gen 3:8). In the end, the gift of God's love, the love of others, and our own love is crippled and nullified, even though it is of unexpected value.

On the contrary, we compulsively strive to be more than what we are: to be right, to be strong, to do everything right, to comply with the rules, to avoid what might be failure or pain, to prove our worth so as to present ourselves before God and others as strong, blameless, demanding, original, dutiful, wise, or without moral failings. In our arrogance, we even believe that we have the right to judge and discriminate harshly against others, like the Pharisee in the parable who failed to experience God's loving justification: "God, I thank you that I am not like other people: thieves, rogues, adulterers, or even like this tax collector. I fast twice a week; I give a tenth of all my income" (Luke 18:11–12).

We hear ourselves in a negative key that is the most radical temptation in our lives: "I am not..."; "I am something bad"; "I am not enough to be liked and loved"; "I am insignificant." The result is that I try to win the affection of others through my efforts. And among others, we include ourselves and God. The temptations of power, of having fun, of being successful, of being highly appreciated are strong, not for their own sake but because they seem to be the desirable and valid way out of the self-rejection we feel and harbor. In this way, we pay attention to the looks, opinions, and benevolent behavior of others to deactivate the negative voices that we believe about ourselves.

All this often happens to us, although we rarely realize it because it has become deeply unconscious through our belief in it. But we get lost and stuck chasing, in so many external places, what is inscribed in our deepest being, waiting to be unfolded only by being sincerely believed. If we are honest, we will soon realize that we spend our energies trying to be the things we do, the things we have, the opinions others have of us, the money we earn, the titles we hold, the social status we are given, the control of the circumstances of life that insist on escaping us, the usefulness we demonstrate, the physical beauty that is not allowed to fade, the intellectual capacities that cannot grow old, the talents we exercise, and the faithful and uncompromising observance of the law or laws we impose on ourselves, especially, for some people, religious laws.

But in the end, none of this can sustain our true self or the value of our lives. As the psalmist says, "For the ransom of life is costly, and can never suffice, that one should live on forever and never see the grave" (Ps 49:8–9).

Nothing can nourish or satisfy us, any more than the pig feed that the younger son in Luke's parable asked for in order not to faint. He, too, had forgotten and ceased to believe that he was still a son and not a servant or a slave (see Luke 15:16, 19). And so, we find ourselves on a constant roller coaster, dizzy from so many meaningless ups and downs: if at times we seem to be devouring the world, at other times we fall into a black hole that brings us crashing down. Our fragility seems to betray us.

Amid it all, God never ceases to call us to be who we are and to live out the vocation to which we have been called, allowing God to be God in our lives. Within us also dwells the voice of God, who will continue to tell us what Jesus heard at his baptism: "This is my Son, the Beloved, with whom I am well pleased" (Matt 3:17). We need to hear it and give it relevance in the face of so many other voices that say the opposite. We need to be able to choose what and who we believe in so that we do not allow ourselves to be manipulated by lies that seduce us; instead, we must take the risk of living in accordance with our true self.

As St. Augustine said in that famous but true phrase: "for

Thou hast formed us for Thyself, and our hearts are restless till they find rest in Thee."[3] Like the two lovers in the Song of Songs, we must persistently seek the true love of our soul until we find it and anchor our soul in a safe harbor.

We know that all true love is a reflection of God. All those who have truly loved us have been human threads of God's love: parents, family members, friends, school and work colleagues, and so many others. Their love has made us realize our value as human beings, given us reason to believe in ourselves, and encouraged us in difficult times.

But we must also remember that only God's love is capable of constantly loving us, of reaching deep within us, of giving us the fullness of love that we seek, and of giving us rest in our deep human restlessness. We must ask for God's love. We must ask to be able to recognize it and to experience it firsthand, even during difficult times when God's face seems to be hidden. We must learn, even if it makes us dizzy, to allow ourselves to be emptied by facing our nakedness and constantly receiving ourselves from the one who created us and who continually recreates us. God alone can ground us in the existential essence of who we are by giving us what we need. Even when the people from whom we most expect love fail us, God will not fail us: "Can a woman forget her nursing child, or show no compassion for the child of her womb? Even these may forget, yet I will not forget you" (Isa 49:15).

The Faith and Temptations of Jesus

Let us now consider how Jesus—our way to the Father, the truth, and life (see John 14:6)—helps us to overcome this radical temptation in order to immerse ourselves in his love.

Jesus lived with the firm conviction that he was the beloved Son, but also in human frailty, with difficulties and temptations. After his experience in the Jordan, the Gospels tell us that he went into the desert where he was tempted. Of the three temptations, in two of the Gospels, two begin with the sentence: "If you are the Son of God..." (Matt 4:3, 6; Luke 4:3, 9).

For Jesus, according to the Gospels, the lying temptation also challenged him with the existential question of his filial identity. It tempted him by cunningly enticing him to prove himself the Son of God and the Savior by turning stones into bread, gaining prestige, and tempting God himself. The temptations of Jesus challenge his being the Son of God, his way of being so, and thus his fundamental identity.

The text of the temptations—both in Luke and Matthew—carries many meanings that are too numerous to cover here. Among them, we underline that in the most vital temptations, both ours and those of Jesus, lurks the essential and vital question of whether we are the beloved daughters and sons of God come what may, or whether we have to do things, accomplish feats, fulfill laws, obtain results and approvals to earn our filial identity, and become children for our own sake. This temptation is an instigation as subtle as it is powerful. Yet, Jesus never let any of these temptations decide for him—even if he was tempted to turn stones into bread to ratify who he was, or to jump out of the temple to gain prestige and get God to intervene. Jesus does not agree because he does not doubt that he is gratuitously and purely the beloved of the Father, even though he feels otherwise, and the temptation is powerful. He does not have to justify who he is because he simply believes and lives by what the Father has said of him.

Jesus always responds to the temptation with the Word of God: "It is written" (Matt 4:4, 8, 12). He answers with the truth of who he is by faithfulness and divine declaration; he does not believe the lie no matter how much it tries to elude his inner self and his beliefs, seducing and deceiving until it distorts the truth. For what "it is written" is true, it is the stable certainty of who God is and who Jesus is, beyond the convincing fickleness of falsehood. This is why Jesus answers, with certainty, that the human being lives from every word that comes from the mouth of God, because it is light, it is life, and through it everything is made (cf. John 1:4).

His life had both moments of difficulty and of success, but neither prevented him from abandoning himself trustingly to the Father.

The temptations did not only occur in the desert at the beginning of Jesus's public life, but they also accompanied him throughout his life and to the cross itself (see Luke 4:13; 22:28; Matt 16:23). At the end of it all, in the face of failure and the most humiliating and devastating absurdity, words like these are hurled at him: "Save yourself! If you are the Son of God, come down from the cross." "He saved others; he cannot save himself. He is the King of Israel; let him come down from the cross now, and we will believe in him. He trusts in God; let God deliver him now, if he wants to; for he said, 'I am God's Son'" (Matt 27:40, 42–43). Even broken and helpless, Jesus trusted, against all evidence and even in the cruel and apparent powerlessness of God, that he was the beloved Son. He believed, against all odds, that this was the way of salvation for many, God's way of salvation. Why did he have to go through such a bitter trial? Why did he have to leave his own? Why did he have to feel the silence of God? Why did he have to go through such a terrible and deadly experience if he wanted to save by loving his own? Why was the way of salvation a hard and existential emptying of self?

Jesus plunges into nothingness, with no support to hold onto in his life, not even the same sensitive protection of God who is either hidden or does not exist. Jesus throws himself with open arms and no return into the dark abyss and total absence, trusting in the God he neither sees nor feels, believing only that God is God, no matter what.

Jesus lives a boundless trust without any other support than his faith. He is accompanied by absurdity, loneliness, abandonment, and silence. Even in the most atrocious bewilderment, Jesus dies with an affirmation of faith on his lips: although he asks why he has been abandoned, he surrenders himself to this God who seems to have been totally eclipsed. Despite this, God is still God, still his God, and the word God speaks remains true, even in the most terrifying existential denial and annihilation. And therefore, Jesus remains the beloved Son who receives himself from God, no matter what happens, until everything is fulfilled, until he dies and God, in whom he trusts, reaffirms him incontestably through the resurrection:

> ...but emptied himself,
>   taking the form of a slave,
>   being born in human likeness.
> And being found in human form...
>
> Therefore God also highly exalted him
>   and gave him the name
>   that is above every name.... (Phil 2:6–11)

In his unstoppable self-giving and love, Jesus saves us in our fragile, tempted, and sinful humanity, "for we do not have a high priest who is unable to sympathize with our weaknesses, but we have one who in every respect has been tested as we are, yet without sin. Let us therefore approach the throne of grace with boldness, so that we may receive mercy and find grace to help in time of need" (Heb 4:15–16).

In Jesus, in his life, death, and resurrection, we have the

certainty of who we are because he has sealed it on the cross. God, through Jesus, has ratified our identity. We cannot doubt the evidence of his love, even amid the darkest trials. Like Paul, we are to ask to believe always with conviction, though we may not always feel it: "I have been crucified with Christ; and it is no longer I who live, but it is Christ who lives in me. And the life I now live in the flesh I live by faith in the Son of God, who loved me and gave himself for me" (Gal 2:19–20).

To Love as We Are Loved

We come to the end of the journey where we have entered into the reality of God's love, from which we emphasize our filial identity, which finds its fullness in Jesus. It is not easy for us to live in this reality because of the existential temptation that makes us doubt our most authentic identity. However, in Jesus we always have the possibility revealed, the confirmation of the inheritance given to us, and the certainty of being loved eternally.

The reality that we are the beloved children of God, but that we doubt this by being alienated from ourselves, has many implications for our lives and especially for our following of Jesus. It is a truth that would merit a much longer and more detailed exposition, because of the interest, scope, and depth that it holds for our human and Christian living. We do not have the space or the time, however, to develop it here, so we will limit ourselves to this brief explanation. Nevertheless, it is essential to recognize how we are affected by self-rejection, since it is the root of all the denial of God in us, of God's love, and, therefore, of our sin.

At the end of this chapter, we are inevitably reminded that our identity of being so loved leads us to the need to love in the same way. Created in the image and likeness of God, we also have an infinite and divine capacity to love: "Love your enemies, do good, and lend, expecting nothing in return. Your reward will be great, and you will be children of the Most High; for he is kind to the ungrateful and the wicked. Be merciful, just as your Father is merciful" (Luke 6:35–36).

Our choices and our way of life can lead us to be more and more who we are, or they can lead us astray from it. If we are daughters and sons, we must learn to live in a way that leads us to affirm and foster our identity, allowing it to unfold and embrace us in our totality through our words, actions, thoughts, and desires, so that it takes full possession of us, floods us, and completely shapes our inner world to the point of overflowing.

However, it would be very childish to remain only in the activity of receiving without giving, thinking that in this way we would be fulfilled. This is another great temptation that seduces us. We believe that we need to beg or demand, coveting the love of others because we lack it and do not know its source. But this is not so: God's love, when received, fills us and overflows us with fullness (cf. Eph 3:17–20). As Jesus taught us, we are complete and deeply fulfilled as persons only when we receive God's love and give it to others, living the first and second commandments in constant rhythm (cf. Matt 22:37–39).

Paul also tells us that we have been set free from the law of sin to serve God: "But now that you have been freed from sin and enslaved to God, the advantage you get is sanctification. The end is eternal life. For the wages of sin is death, but the free gift of God is eternal life in Christ Jesus our Lord" (Rom 6:22–23).

It is a matter of allowing ourselves to be loved as Jesus allowed himself to be loved by the Father, so that we may love with the same love with which we are loved (cf. John 15:12). This is the freedom to which Christ calls us, the freedom to serve others: "For you were called to freedom, brothers and sisters; only do not use your freedom as an opportunity for self-indulgence, but through love become slaves to one another. For the whole law is summed up in a single commandment, 'You shall love your neighbor as yourself'" (Gal 5:13–14).

Jesus asks us to abide in him and in his love, just as he abides in the Father and in the love of God. This creates in us, without error, the dynamism to love as he loved us, giving his life for his friends (cf. John 15:13). He always wants to wash our feet so that we may do the same for one another (cf. John 13:13–15, 34–35). He serves us so that we may learn to serve as we are served (cf. Matt 20:26–28; Luke 22:26–27).

What a vital task and, at the same time, one so out of our reach because it is only possible with his help. Only in this way can we become who we already are, but not yet fully. Our human existence is a call to develop our true self in a progressive and transcendent process. It is a path of growth that is already present in the form of seeds but needs to be constantly unfolded until we reach our full maturity in Christ through love (cf. Eph 4:13).

3

A Pedagogy for Freedom

Now that we have marked out points under the panorama of God's love, it is time to outline the way to the goal: we want to present paths of truth in God so that we let ourselves be liberated and strengthened by love until we choose to love as God does.

The aim of this chapter is to explore the real, pedagogical ways so that God's love, addressed in the second chapter, can permeate our land as outlined in the first chapter. How can we allow God's love to penetrate every single space of our daily life, without impermeable, intrusive, and hidden defenses, without hiding anything from God, and defying the resistant fears that close us off and make us flee from God's presence?

Following the same existential coordinates of the first chapter, we will begin with some pedagogical hints that weave through this chapter: letting God be God in us; our vulnerability; the need for prayer as a space for grace; discernment and spiritual accompaniment; and coming closer to the person of Jesus.

Beginning the Journey

Letting God Be God in Us

Throughout life, it is essential to let God be God in us. We need to allow God to enter into all that we are, for only he can transform us with love and grace. Even in our personal reality, God's will is revealed when we pay attention to our passions, impulses, needs, and all our inner movements. If we learn to interpret ourselves, we will welcome God's manifestation through our frailty and indigence. Fidelity to God's work of art—that is, each one of us—demands that we allow God to be in our specific originality and limitation.

Our freedom requires a radical belief in that small portion of God within us, the source of our originality and our being. It is not necessary to disregard anything; rather, we must embrace everything as that exclusive *mina* that is given to us as a possibility of life and fulfillment in God (cf. Luke 19:11–27). We are to make it yield beyond our paralyzing and discouraging fears that, by lying, bury us (cf. Matt 25:25). Each of us is a mystery that needs to be deciphered. The code to such an enigma lies in radical fidelity to what is within each of us. Although we cannot affirm that everything in us is good, we can discover in everything how God is present and wants to act: "We know that all things work together for good for those who love God, who are called according to his purpose" (Rom 8:28).

As we saw in the second chapter, this is not easy, because we believe in the fallacy of discarding who we are. We make the mistake of running away from our shame by seeking an unreal beauty. One of the dangers in the spiritual process lies in wanting to identify ourselves with ideals—good in themselves—without attending to our own limitations or weaknesses. The danger is to think that, because we profess them, they are already integrated and have transformed our being. But this is not so; this is not enough. To remain only in the spiritualistic or theoretical profession of values and principles fragments us inwardly to the point of even making us sick. It makes us delusional without being grounded. Because we find it difficult to admit with humility that we do not live according to the ideal, we deceive ourselves and justify our inconsistencies. We may project our inadequacy onto others, judging them harshly because they do not live according to the goals we proclaim, without realizing that we do not do so either (cf. Matt 7:3–5). Our false self will make us intransigent toward ourselves and project this intransigence even onto God. Or it will cause us to give up, to abandon all hope.

We need to remember, again and again, that it is only in the certainty that God is not scandalized by anything of who we are that we can with abandonment and security dare to touch our inconsistencies. It is in our most secret room, in our uniqueness and peculiarity, that God sees us and waits, to give us light, to love us unconditionally, and to be our reward (cf. Matt 6:4, 6, 18). We must ask the Spirit to thwart fear and shame from preventing us from entering God's presence.

Sensations, thoughts, feelings, needs, and others can and need to be visited, known, and recognized with and by God. In the *kairos* of each moment, Jesus tells us, like Zacchaeus: "Hurry and come down; for I must stay at your house today" (Luke 19:5). Let us ask to joyfully welcome him in our humble truth, so that our prayer may embrace our whole life and embrace us completely.

We Are Vulnerable

Self-acceptance recognizes the true self-image, lowers defenses, and removes lies. Note that the greater the experience of God's love, the greater the experience of our own vulnerability, limitation, and sin. We will recognize ourselves as vulnerable—that is, susceptible to being hurt—with the temptation to defend ourselves, attack, hide, or run away. It may seem that, instead of moving forward in the way of God and love, we are getting stuck more and more in our own mud. It is important to know where this journey is taking us so that we are not deceived or frightened, and do not retreat for lack of clarity or perseverance.

Learning to live out of God's love presupposes a progressive, difficult, and uncomfortable self-emptying that is, nevertheless, inevitable. Love strips us naked and empties us so as to fill us, making us what we were created to be: a radical reception of God who lowers himself to serve us (cf. Luke 22:26–27; Phil 2:6–8).

God lets us know: "My grace is sufficient for you, for power is made perfect in weakness" (2 Cor 12:9). We need to believe in the power of grace in our lowliness. We need to remain helpless before God, open to the beauty of love, to its inexhaustible depth and persistence. God will give us the audacity to confront the truth about ourselves and our self-deception. Welcoming this grace into our fragile reality is the only way to God, as the saint of Assisi said: "Holiness is not a self-fulfillment, nor a self-given fullness. It is above all an emptiness that is discovered and accepted, and which God comes to fill to the extent that one opens oneself to God's fullness. You see, our nothingness, if accepted, becomes the free space in which God can still create."[1]

Prayer and Grace Are Indispensable

Prayer is making space and time for God. Only when God nourishes us is it possible to follow the way, because for us it would be too long and even impossible (cf. 1 Kings 19:7; Mark 10:27).

Prayer gives us life; it enables us to remember and listen to God. It awakens the memory of our heart and nourishes our affectivity. Prayer is born and opens space for grace, which does in us what we are not able to ask or even imagine (cf. Eph 3:21).

There are as many ways to pray as there are people. We are all different, with different sensitivities and characteristics, and so we should pray in our own original way. In any case, without forgetting the sacramental and liturgical means that the Church gives us, it is essential and irreplaceable to devote exclusive time to God, nourished by the Word, in the personal silence of our being to welcome God.

Although there is a great variety of forms of prayer in the Church, there are fundamental aspects that can help. For this reason, throughout the chapter, we will include pedagogical proposals for prayer, offering suggestions on how to let God meet us in each interior space.

In our Christian journey, it is not enough to know ourselves so that we are automatically able to love as Jesus did. It is not enough to recognize what is wrong, what needs to be changed in us, or what needs to be empowered so that we can do it on our own. We need grace to work in us with our consent, to enable us. As St. Augustine wrote: "Therefore he who made you without you does not justify you without you....But it is he who justifies."[2]

Pope Francis reminds us that we can only allow God to transform us through a "heartfelt and prayerful acknowledgment of our limitations." Without this, we make transformation impossible: the lack of this recognition "prevents grace from working more effectively within us, for no room is left for bringing about the potential good that is part of a sincere and genuine journey of growth" (*Gaudete et Exsultate*, 50).

"Can I not do with you, O house of Israel, just as this potter has done? says the LORD. Just like the clay in the potter's hand, so are you in my hand, O house of Israel" (Jer 18:6). The question God asks is not "Why don't you do it on your own?" "Why don't you transform yourselves?" Not even "Why don't you fix the clay that breaks and spoils in your hands?" The great question of God, in the potter's house, is "Can I not do with you what this potter does?" Unfortunately, we often think and believe that we are the ones who need to do it by our own will, by our own strength, and by fulfilling the rules, forgetting that prayer is about letting God do the work.

Mary of Nazareth did not respond to the angel's annunciation that she would do it. Her answer was a consent, a request, an open space for grace. She asked God to accomplish in her what had been announced to her: "Here am I, the servant of the Lord; let it be with me according to your word" (Luke 1:38). In the same way, we are to place ourselves before God and ask that, with our consent, our availability, and our will, God will carry out the work begun in us (cf. Phil 1:6). It is essential that we live in the open, unprotected before God, who takes possession of us and fulfills the promise to make us God's own.

Discernment and Spiritual Accompaniment

All that we have been talking about is to be included and to be put side by side with that great richness of the Christian tradition, which is discernment. To distinguish and to know what dwells within us, to call movements by name, to be enlightened by grace, to choose in freedom, and to live in the light is part of this process that Christian spirituality proposes to us.

To discern, we need to discover our own chords and those of God, in our inner symphony. We also need to be liberated by mercy to choose which chords to play and which to mute.

The Church's tradition on discernment helps, enriches, and complements what is addressed here. We will make explicit reference to some of its valuable teachings where necessary. What we are about to say, on the one hand, participates in and enriches the art of discernment, and on the other hand, it presupposes and needs it. For the great difficulty in discernment often comes not from the supposed remoteness of God but from the remoteness of ourselves. That is why we want to provide more interior elements so that we can discern with greater insight.

Another of the great riches of our Christian tradition is the need for spiritual accompaniment. The journey of personal knowledge of God can only be made in the company of those who go before us. All that has been said so far, and all that is to come, can be read from a personal perspective, as well as from the accompaniment received or given to others. The contents of this book are an enrichment to that essential tool which is the accompaniment of the spiritual life of others.

Getting Closer to the Person of Jesus

Another of our goals that we will pursue briefly is to approach the person of Jesus from the same coordinates through which we enter our inner world. We will look at the sensations, the thoughts, the feelings, the needs, the affections, the desires, the will, the choices, and the actions of the Man-God of Nazareth in the Gospels. It is urgent to be able to look at Jesus more and more, not only from a dogmatic and intellectual perspective but also from the most human and natural one of trivial life. The theology we are used to is essentially rational, systematic, made up of doctrines and dogmas. Instead, we urgently need a theology that addresses our existential, emotional, and affective questions. In Christology, we look at Jesus as the incarnate Logos with his two natures and his christological titles, but we do not look at his affectivity and his way of living his inner movements. This is also essential for our salvation.

This is a fundamental question that will lead us to know Jesus in a more credible way, by discovering him in a more human and therefore more divine way. Knowing ourselves enables us to know him. Knowing him, in his revelation, enables us to know ourselves in a more human way, in his image and likeness, beloved daughters and sons, realizing that we are made of the same human clay, and that in the same way we can be greatly blessed by God (cf. Heb 4:15).

If we look at him and welcome him in a more human way, we will allow his humanity to reveal itself, to assume us and to save us. It is a matter of walking with him through the dusty streets of life, risking that he will ask us: "But who do you say that I am?" (Matt 16:15). We will approach his body and his interiority to touch and see, to hear and smell, to taste and know the Word of life and to believe in the Logos of God who became fragile flesh and dwelt among us (cf. John 1:14; 1 John 1:1–4).

Let us now move on to revisit our inner spaces.

Walking Together with God

Let us embark on this inner journey with the certainty that someone is with us, calling us from within, to fulfill us. Let us ask for the necessary grace to be transformed by the fire of God's love.

Sensing God

The verb *to sense* has a very deep meaning in English and is not easy to translate in other languages. *To sense* speaks of the sensations experienced by the body. At the same time, it means to feel, to think, to intuit, to understand, to perceive, to apprehend, to have the impression of, to be aware of, and so on.

Sensing God suggests that welcoming God in us involves the body with all its capacities of perception. The body is the sacred ground where God's presence is manifested, and, for this reason, it is the tent of encounter and relationship with the Lord. It is our house of prayer because we are the temple of the Spirit (cf. Exod 33:7, 11; Isa 56:7; 1 Cor 6:19).

Although it seems to be an unpopular terrain in traditional Christian spirituality, and even today, the encounter with God happens through the inevitable encounter with each one of us in our corporeality, and not by ignoring, rejecting, or alienating ourselves from it.

Enjoying our corporeality

It is in the ways of worldly and corporeal life that the divine is at play, reaching out to us and expressing itself through our sensoriality. This is neither epidermal nor frivolous. We cannot fall into the misconception that the body is only sinful or alien to the sacred. God embraces us with love, even and especially in our bodies, in our fragile and limited flesh: "Then the glory of the LORD shall be revealed, and all people shall see it together, for the mouth of the LORD has spoken" (Isa 40:5).

The human body is a mine of spirituality, with an immense wealth to be recovered. It is the place par excellence of the revelation of God made man, flesh and body (cf. John 1:14). We will only radically accept the humanity of Jesus if we take our corporeality seriously, because he consciously and voluntarily assumed it. If we reject our corporeality, we deny his incarnation. Learning to value our corporeality as a gift from God is essential for our lives.

Drawing close to God necessarily leads us to stumble upon the perimeter of our sensibility, which is shaped by our senses and sensations. And will this not be *con-templating*? Is this not being with (*con*) the sacred (*temple*) that we are and carry with us wherever we go? To contemplate can never be to abandon reality, but to let ourselves be affected by what surrounds us, to be attentive to the echoes that reach us—the fruit of both external and internal sensitive impacts. To receive God in everything and to re-encounter the divinity in its depth means welcoming the divine through our senses:

- learning to keep your eyes open, as the biblical author states God does: "I have observed the misery of my people who are in Egypt; I have heard their cry on account of their taskmasters. Indeed, I know their sufferings" (Exod 3:7);
- insisting, therefore, on keeping one's ears open to know the reality;
- to savor life with its pleasures without shunning the bitterness it also brings us, drinking from the great and small chalices (cf. Ps 23:5; Mark 10:38–39);
- to remain awake and in contact with what touches our skin, aware of the vital cold and warmth that many experience (cf. Luke 7:37–50); and
- wanting to smell the fundamental aromas that envelop us without being able to stop or evade them (cf. John 12:3).

It is urgent that we are awakened by our own senses amid the continuous bombardment of overcommunication that seeks to anesthetize, overload, and numb us. The asceticism of the senses does not only mean abandoning the sensitive and noisy world. There are many things that go unnoticed because we are immersed in various chores, rush, anxiety, and mental inquiry that often rob us of our contemplative and sensitive availability. We cannot forget the magnetic power of our cell phones that kidnap us from the here and now, surrounding us at every moment, and transport us to a distant virtual world. Nor can we be naive about the internet that, while useful and necessary, can overwhelm us and rob us of our privacy. This very important reality deserves attention because we cannot underestimate how the use of new technologies changes our behavior, abilities, relationships, use of time, and so on. For many people, it goes so far as to become an addiction, bearing the signs of a real vice: discomfort, anxiety, lack of control, and even social and mental disorders.

Inquiring God in sensations

What was printed on our immemorial photographic film needs to be developed. Today, almost all photography is digital. Once upon a time, the film was imprinted in the patient secrecy of the camera until a special dim light developed those images on paper in a darkroom. Similarly, we need to give space and time to create the "darkroom" within ourselves where the traces of reality engraved in us through the senses can be imprinted in our sensations and revealed in our consciousness.

Silences are essential in learning to be attentive to what inhabits us, the fruit of what surrounds, impresses, and invades us. Likewise, the meaning of silence, even when it means quiet moments, is not always the absence of noise but rather radical openness, reverent awareness, and attentive presence to reality. Life and God are not reserved only for quiet moments. The divine is always here, meeting us through everything and everyone. If we tune in, we will welcome God. This is a prayerful life (cf. Eph 6:18): getting used to encountering ourselves, others, and God in the calls of existence amid the deserts of the city. Praying throughout life challenges us to discover the whisper of God both in the natural sounds of creation as well as in the noises made by human beings.

But how do we do all this? One way is to give citizenship back to our senses and answer the simplest of questions: What have I seen, heard, touched, smelled, and tasted? We can answer when our sensibility is affected, or we can wait until we enter that darkroom—made of respectful time and intimate space—that we cannot renounce.

Another question to answer is: What sensations does my body have in response to what I have experienced? To answer this question, the list of sensations we outlined in the first chapter can help.[3] After discovering so many impacts, consequences of reality, we should continue to inquire: Where are you, my God, amid all that I am experiencing?

We will be surprised to see how God meets us in so many sensorial experiences that we often overlook:

- The smile that awaited you when you met a friend again, where God hinted the value of fidelity
- The expression of suffering of so many people on television that made you feel disturbed and demanding justice
- The illness that knocked at your door that made you experience pain and absurdity, the weakness that made you fragile and made you cry out the existential question of life's meaning

- That cool beer on a hot summer afternoon that made you grateful for thirst and for the drink that quenched it
- The smell of wet earth after the rain that brought you to the certainty of providence, which rains on everyone, good and bad
- The tiredness we experience in the face of situations we cannot control, whether a pandemic or so many wars, that speak of our human fragility
- Staring at the full moon at night that indicates a light beyond the darkness because it reflects the sun even when we can no longer see it
- The feeling of relaxation after physical exercise that says we must also take care of ourselves when stress presses on

All these, and many other examples, can be those unseen but certain footsteps of God. If we are attentive, we can hear God knocking at the door of our sensorial realities (cf. Rev 3:20). Let us ask to learn to distinguish God's signs (cf. Matt 16:1–3). Let us ask God to liberate us from within so that we may be attentive to our interiority through the awareness of our *sensing*. Let us ask to learn the prayerful silence that creates time and space for God alone, a silence that can also find God in the hectic ups and downs of life.

How did Jesus live the relationship with the body?

All of Jesus's relationships are through corporeality and never through a disembodied spirituality. This is how Jesus reveals the face of God to us: he takes the risk of a "body to body" encounter with others, with the faces of many people whose physical presence is full of pain and suffering.

One of Jesus's earliest miracles in the Gospel is the healing of a leper: "A leper came to him begging him, and kneeling he said to him, 'If you choose, you can make me clean.' Moved with pity, Jesus stretched out his hand and touched him, and said to him, 'I do choose. Be made clean!' Immediately the leprosy left him, and he was made clean" (Mark 1:40–42). It is remarkable to contemplate the conversation of these two characters through their bodily movements. A leper, breaking the Jewish law by being unclean recognizes in Jesus the dignity of a priest (see Lev 13), comes to him, and brings his body, just like that, into his presence. The leper, with his smell, with his appearance, with his risk of contagion, with his disease, was certainly very uncomfortable to be with. But Jesus expresses acceptance and love in a physical way: he does not move away, he welcomes, listens, touches, and says: "I do choose. Be made clean!" (Mark 1:41). Jesus manifests God's compassion because he has certainly experienced it from others and from the Father, in his own body as well.

Jesus contemplated life and nature, he let himself be steeped in God's loving providence, and he draws our attention to it: "Consider the lilies, how they grow: they neither toil nor spin..." (Luke 12:27). The rhythm of nature spoke to him of God and his care.

We are invited to read the Gospel from a physical perspective—from the body language, from the senses and the sensations. How fascinating it would be to go through all the chapters of the Gospel simply by paying attention to the body and the senses. And to perceive the body as the place par excellence where love is received, expressed, and revealed. So much so that without the body we would not have known the incarnate eternal love: "This is my body, which is given for you. Do this in remembrance of me" (Luke 22:19; cf. 1 John 1:1–2).

Thinking of God Who Thinks of Us

Having recognized our sensations, we now access our inner self by noticing our thoughts. It is through them that we interpret the external and internal influences that reach us. The section on thoughts that we discussed in the first chapter can help here.

Our thoughts are shaped by our upbringing, our own family and social values. We have many ideals, prejudices, cultural norms, ideas, implicit and explicit laws, prohibitions, rights, duties, and so on, of which we are often not even aware. Some of these may already be the fruit of the Gospel in us, but many of them still are not.

Knowing what we think

Knowing what we are thinking is a way of being able to accept what God is saying to us, because God also communicates with us through our thoughts. But since not all our thoughts—even those that seem the most holy and pious—are inspired by God, we must be attentive to discern them and discover how the Creator is present and communicating through them. We must contrast his way of thinking with our own to achieve conversion and transformation of mind. It takes a delicate insight given to us by the Spirit to discern what is his and what is not. God forewarns us: "For my thoughts are not your thoughts, nor are your ways my ways, says the LORD. For as the heavens are higher than the earth, so are my ways higher than your ways and my thoughts than your thoughts" (Isa 55:8–9).

Accepting God's way of thinking and following Jesus implies a change of mind. After the first announcement of the Passion and the confirmation of his mission, Jesus harshly rebukes Peter for not accepting the foreseen cruel end of his life: "Get behind me, Satan! You are a stumbling block to me; for you are setting your mind not on divine things but on human things" (Matt 16:23). Accepting the ways of Jesus means acquiring a new mentality according to God's way (cf. Rom 12:2).

At every step, there is a loving and sincere confrontation that takes us beyond ourselves and saves us from ourselves. Sin and self-rejection lead us astray, make us miss the goal and miss the mark, for they make us call good something that is bad and bad something that is good. We need to recognize the deceptions, subtleties, justifications, fallacies, errors, and misunderstandings that arise from our false belief that we are not loved for who we are. St. Ignatius warns us that sometimes, even with the best of intentions, we start out thinking well and from God, but without realizing it, we end up thinking badly and departing from his ways.

If we remain obstinate in thoughts contrary to God's, they will lead us to destruction (cf. John 10:10), to disaster, and never to full realization and communion.

Letting ourselves be transformed in our thoughts

How can our thoughts be more and more transformed by God?

Prayer is a constitutive part of this journey, because it brings us before God with our thoughts so that they may be confirmed or radically renewed by the Holy Spirit (cf. Rom 8:26–27). Through prayer, we need to try to answer the questions of what we think and why we think what we think, so we can recognize our thoughts in the face of the vicissitudes that occur to us. We must ask to be known: "Prove me, O LORD, and try me; test my heart and mind. For your steadfast love is before my eyes, and I walk in faithfulness to you" (Ps 26:2–3; cf. Ps 139:1–4). Enlightened by God's Word, we should ask: And what do you think, Lord? To pray is to aspire to have the mind of God, even when it seems to be foolishness and error.

The profound freedom to which God wants to lead us is to think with and like him, when his ways are attractive to us and when they are totally unexpected, difficult, and unusual. God will always respect us and will not force us against our will. God will accompany us until we see that his plans for us are of happiness and peace, even when they sometimes seem to be quite the opposite (cf. Jer 29:11–13).

Learning to think with Jesus

On his journey, Jesus allowed himself to be shaped by God's Word and way of thinking. He allowed himself to be inwardly modeled by his mercy and knowledge. But he did not allow himself to be shaped by wrong interpretations of religion, such as discrimination, hypocrisy, and injustice in the name of God (see Matt 5:7; 12:7; 23:23). Nor did he allow himself to be led astray by misguided messianic expectations that diverted him from God's way of saving (see Matt 4:1–11; 16:21–23; John 6:14–15). However, he also allowed the faith of others to transform his way of thinking (see Matt 15:22–28). Amid the ups and downs of life, Jesus sought the Father's thoughts about himself, about others, and about the direction of existence (see Luke 9:28, 35; John 12:26–28).

Like him, we can be converted to what God thinks of us and of others so that we do not get stuck in distorted and lying images. With Jesus, we are to "think of God who thinks of us" and keep the meaning of his words, until we accept his plans and follow him in his ways. A pedagogy of prayer so that we may become ever more rooted in God's love is to think and meditate often on our filial identity, even if our thoughts do not always confirm it and our feelings contradict it. As Henri Nouwen noted, "I am firmly convinced that the decisive moment of Jesus's public life was his baptism, when he heard the divine affirmation, 'You are my Beloved on whom my favor rests.'…There is in each of us an inner voice of Love that says: 'You are the Beloved of God!' I want you to claim your Belovedness. You don't have to get caught in searches that lead nowhere....You can choose to reach out now for true inner freedom and find it ever more fully."[4]

Our thoughts have an immense power in us because they lead us to the goal that we consider to be good and meaningful. We cannot forget that thought is a driving force in our inner world. It is worth remembering the following lines in *The Iron Lady*, a movie about Margaret Thatcher's life, in which she vehemently affirms the vital dynamism of thoughts: "Watch your thoughts, for they become words. Watch your words, for they become actions. Watch your actions, for they become habits. Watch your habits, for they become your character. And watch your character, for it becomes your destiny. What we think, we become. My father always said that."[5]

God is also always telling us who we are, so that by thinking about it we can become more and more what God thinks about us and makes us think about ourselves: our true identity.

Feeling in God

Let us now go down to the level of feelings. There is a certain tendency to contrast thoughts with feelings. Both, however, are important and bring us closer to the truth within, and both perspectives need to be considered. Thoughts tell us about the ideals we pursue and formulate, what we perceive as the direction and values of our lives. Feelings tell us whether what we profess is really a coherent echo of our whole being; they reveal our actual adherence to what we think.

We may have a good, spiritual thought, but it may be accompanied by conflicting feelings of resistance. In this case, we must ask ourselves: What is inwardly opposing this idea?

What is resisting this spiritual proposal? What is emotionally preventing me from adhering to what I consider good? Consequently, we can see if there is a specific resistance that needs a process of purification, or if it indicates that we are going in the opposite direction of the good to which we are called.

As we discussed in the first chapter's section on feelings, they can frighten us because we cannot control them, they elude our determination, and they can even be the opposite of what we would like to feel. Sometimes they say what we don't want to hear but should still listen to. It is also true that, at many times and on many occasions, they confirm what we think and add a pleasant color to life. In other moments, however, feelings come and go quickly and fleetingly without being too relevant, and so they should not be given too much weight. Learning to recognize and distinguish our emotions will allow them to translate and reveal our true experiences—the good, the bad, the pleasant, the unpleasant, the attractive, and the repulsive. Our emotional reality reveals what we are attracted to and what we reject in the Gospel, in ourselves, and in others. It will also show the depth of our inner conversion: the extent to which we identify with the feelings of Christ (cf. Phil 2:5). Therefore, the emotional realm, although it may seem unruly and impetuous, needs to be touched and evangelized by God. But how? What do we do with feelings? How do we live with them? How can we allow God to find us, love us, and transform us in our emotions?

We dare to say that this is one of the most difficult challenges we have, for we are afraid to embrace our most disconcerting feelings that seem to confirm that we are not worthy of being loved, not even by God. Even more arduous is to place ourselves with them before God. I will pay more attention to talking about the feelings that most unsettle us, because we do not struggle with those that are more pleasant. I will present five moments:

- welcoming feelings
- feeling them
- recognizing and naming them
- interpreting where they come from and where they are pushing us to
- deciding what to do

Welcoming feelings

The first step is to cultivate a welcoming attitude toward feelings, granting them dignity by acknowledging their right to exist within us—to welcome them without fear, without judgment, without condemnation, without justification, and without evasion.

Usually, when we become aware of our less pleasant feelings, we tend to get scared and enter a state of alarm, believing that we are in danger or in trouble. The first step is to resist being carried away by fright and avoid feeding it.

It is also important not to judge the situations or people we think are responsible for our feelings. Even more, we should try not to judge ourselves for what we feel. We tend to judge ourselves according to the goodness or badness we attribute to the feelings: "How come I still feel this way at my age?"; "If I were a good person I would feel differently"; "I pray so much and I feel what I shouldn't"; "Why can't I control my feelings?"; "If God had power in me, I wouldn't feel this way"; and so on.

Condemnation stems from judgment. If I believe that I shouldn't feel what I'm feeling, I attribute condemnations or verdicts to myself, even if they are false: "I'm bad," "I'm guilty," "I'm not good," "I'll never do better," "I'm worthless," "What an idiot," "I can't," "I deserve punishment," "I'm incapable," "Go away," "Shut up," "I have to prove myself," "I'm useless," "I don't do anything right," "I'm beyond saving," and so on. It is here, through emotional resonances, that we can most clearly discover the echoes of self-rejection within us, in the judgments we often make of ourselves. But we don't need to condemn ourselves for having them.

Sometimes, however, to prevent ourselves from going within, we start to justify ourselves: "If only...." "If only that person had not said that...." Justification attempts to absolve us of responsibility for what we feel, taking away a supposed guilt. But justifying ourselves hinders us from welcoming our feelings.

There is another attitude: running away, trying to avoid the emotions we feel. But sooner or later, we will encounter them again. Neither avoidance nor denial resolves the situation. Thinking that time fixes everything doesn't always work, and even less so in this case.

The best thing to do is to accept the feelings, wherever they come from, whatever their burden, or whatever they say. If they knock on the door, open it politely. Be it anger or tenderness, indignation or admiration. We are to welcome them with magnanimity as an integral part of our lives.

Nor is it worth fighting them to weaken or eliminate them. They are stronger and more persistent. They are a psychodynamic energy that needs to be expressed, released, until it fades away. Only by attending to them will we go through the necessary process of getting to know them, listening to them, and allowing them to calm down by offering us their psychic energy. This does not mean that we identify ourselves with them; they are ours, but they are not who we are.

We are to welcome them, to let them be, to pay attention to them so as to recognize them, even if it is uncomfortable. By savoring them even when they are pleasant, we can enjoy more of the inner beauty they offer us, which we often neglect.

Feeling the feelings

A second step is to feel them. This does not mean acting on our feelings or being carried in the direction they are pushing us. It is about getting in touch with them, with their energy and meaning.

How do you feel them? Acknowledge them and pay attention to what you feel. Let their energy express itself inwardly in words, images, movements, or silence. Engaging in artistic expressions like music, drawing, painting, or writing can be helpful. Vigorous exercise can be another option, as it allows the body to release inner energy in a healthy way. For others, feeling goes through other activities, such as cooking, chopping wood, driving, fishing, talking, and so on. The important thing is not to do anything dangerous for anyone, but to do something useful.

It is important to remain present and in touch with what is happening inside without wanting to fix or change what you are feeling. We just need to keep feeling. Nor can we put an expiration date on feelings. They will tell us how long they need; some come and go, but the more persistent feelings require our attention. We will know when they no longer have power over us.

Feelings can and should be felt in the presence of God. It is about bringing together God's presence and our emotional world. Letting them be, feeling with God. Prayer is about allowing God to meet us where we are with our emotions, without us having to change them. It is God who reaches out and touches our feelings in unexpected ways, enlightening us to understand what is happening and changing us if necessary. It is up to us to place ourselves in his hands so that he can do with us and our feelings as he sees fit. Moreover, if we consider that emotions also come from our subconscious, it is even more difficult to control them and even more necessary to feel them in the presence of God.

In prayer, we are invited to feel what we feel, to wait on God as if we were in an "emotional massage." It is useless to try to push the emotion away, even if the temptation is great. God embraces us with our feelings, and we embrace him. God reaches out to us. It does not matter if we feel better or worse, bad or good; the important thing is to feel and wait in faith before God with the feelings that inhabit us. He transforms us, unites us with himself and loves us even in the most emotionally uncomfortable silence, pacifying us and giving us light on what is happening to us.

The same, with equal intensity, applies to pleasant feelings arising in us. To feel them in the silence of prayer makes them even more precious, consoles us, unites us with God, and strengthens us from within. It would be a pity if we did not take advantage of the "good" feelings to enjoy them more within ourselves and with God. Too often we end up enjoying consolations too little, trying only to escape the desolations.

Recognizing and naming feelings

To feel our feelings and understand what is happening within us, it is necessary to try to name them. It is not always easy to identify them. Often, we feel constellations of conflicting and contradictory emotions, mixed with thoughts, sensations, and other inner spaces that are difficult to distinguish. But as much as possible, we will get used to recognizing what we are feeling by giving a name to what is happening.

The question to answer is: What am I feeling? The list presented in the first chapter can help us answer this question.[6]

However, how we answer this question doesn't always reflect what we are feeling, which can often betray us. When we are asked, "What do you feel?" we frequently respond with thoughts, judgments, or behaviors, either our own or those of others. When we answer this question with sentences beginning with "I feel that...," "I feel as if...," or "I feel that you...," we are probably expressing thoughts instead of feelings: "I think that...," "I think as if...," "I think that you...." Changing the verbs gives us more clarity.

There are also other expressions that we can call "false feelings" because they again express thoughts that contain judgments about behavior. This group includes words following the words "I feel": I feel abandoned, abused, harassed, threatened, attacked, trapped, censored, coerced, discredited, neglected, despised, unprotected, dominated, deceived, cheated, excluded, exploited, humiliated, ignored, misunderstood, undervalued, insulted, bullied, judged, manipulated, unloved, forgotten, pressured, rejected, ridiculed, betrayed, used, and so on.

To say that these words do not express feelings but rather behaviors or evaluations of actions made by me or others does not mean that they are not emotionally charged, unimportant, or inexpressive of real actions. The words can accurately reflect a situation, judge what is happening, but refrain from describing a feeling or helping to feel it. Beyond the judgments that may be true or false, right or wrong, we need to discover the real feelings and sensations they evoke and carry. If we try to get in touch with our feelings through these words instead of feeling and releasing their energy, we increase the inner emotional charge by remembering the action that triggered the feelings according to our interpretation. So we get ourselves into a vicious and painful cycle. What the person then does is to focus more on what has happened instead of focusing on what he or she is really feeling, thereby reinforcing the cause of the feeling, continually rekindling its fire instead of letting it burn until it fades.

To the question "What am I feeling?" we must try to find adequate answers that express emotions, however uncomfortable they may be. Only then will we own our emotional world and not be owned by it. Here, too, the grace of God through the Word, with its light and insight, is essential (cf. Heb 4:12).

Interpreting where feelings come from and where they go

We must also try to perceive what has caused the feelings we are experiencing and where they are taking us. It is about interpreting what they are telling me.

This helps us to understand our emotional responses to life's stimuli. It also enables us to distinguish whether what our feelings are asking us to do is consistent with how we want to live or not, and why. Feelings give us a lot of information; they can be echoes of God in the person. For example, a person may feel anger about a situation that is deeply unjust in his or her life or in the lives of others. Through this anger, God may be indicating that the injustice committed needs to be confronted in some way and that the person needs to do something about the situation. It may also indicate that some aspects of the personality need to be addressed rather than suppressed, as is often the case.

In this circumstance, interpreting where the anger is coming from and where it is going help the person to get in touch with the inner source of their energy and get closer to the Spirit of God. This feeling reveals the inner world and leads to God who wants to give life. Anger then becomes an expression of God's defense and desire. To reject anger, here, would mean to reject a valuable source of information. To welcome it, to feel it, and to interpret it, however, creates space for the divine life to flourish and to come alive within.

It is essential to interpret the emotions that we experience to discern whether they lead us in the right direction, according to the gospel, or whether they lead us to withdraw selfishly into ourselves. Interpreting inner movements requires patience, attention, and honest confrontation with the Word of God and the moral demands of the Christian life.

Lord, what do we do?

Everything we have said so far through these levels is already part of prayer. This fifth level involves specifically deciding with God what to do and how to do it, based on what we're feeling. We will talk more about this later in the next section under the heading "Deciding in Freedom."[7]

Getting closer to Jesus's feelings

We conclude this section by drawing closer to the feelings of Jesus. We will identify paths to know him under this unique and seldom heard perspective, even though it is a fundamental dimension of his life. We are compelled to journey through stories of the gospel, appreciating the way he lived his emotions and engaged with those of others. In the Gospels, there are several verbs that speak to us about Jesus's affections in a rich and diverse way. Approaching Jesus in his way of living the multifaceted richness of the emotional world will give us many clues. All these levels that we have addressed above—and much more—can also be glimpsed in various scenes of his life. We will explicitly mention some, by way of example. Jesus embraced and felt his feelings, including compassion, anger, and joy: "He looked around at them with anger; he was grieved at their hardness of heart and said to the man..." (Mark 3:5; cf. Mark 1:41; Luke 10:21). He recognized the feelings and gave them a name: amid the people who had been with him for three days (see Matt 15:32), in the certainty of his love for his own (see John 15:9), and in the imminence of his passion:

"He took with him Peter and James and John, and began to be distressed and agitated. And he said to them, 'I am deeply grieved, even to death; remain here, and keep awake'" (Mark 14:33–34). Jesus interpreted where the feelings were coming from and where they were going, and decided with God what to do; he rejoiced deeply in the Holy Spirit, who spoke to him about how God acts (see Luke 10:21); he loved the one who asked him what to do but did not follow him on the way (see Mark 10:21); continued to go up to Jerusalem even in the anxious expectation of what would happen to him there (see Luke 12:50); still shared the last supper with his disciples on the night when he was to be betrayed (see Luke 22:40–44); waited for some days in the face of the serious illness of his friend (see John 11:5–7); was aware of his grave responsibility at the farewell supper with his own (see John 13:1–3); committed himself and entrusted all in his prayer to his Father (see John 17:23, 26), and so on.

Jesus cared for his emotional world as a fundamental part of the stage where human life open to God unfolds. He did not discard anything he felt and allowed it all to serve as a springboard, not a trap, for the sacred. He lived healthily with his own feelings and approached, touched, and welcomed the feelings of those hoping for his mercy who crossed paths with him (see Mark 5:33; 9:6; Luke 10:17; 13:17). Today, at the edges of our history, he also welcomes us with our emotions, until, by his hand, we can share his feelings (cf. Phil 2:5; Col 3:12–15).

Recognizing Our Needs Before God

As explained in the initial chapter, our needs manifest through the emotions that we experience, as they indicate to us whether one or more needs are being met or not. Just as with emotions, it is important to welcome, recognize, and name our needs within us, enabling us to provide them with appropriate responses.[8]

Living healthily with our needs requires us to know them and make them explicit; to take personal responsibility for them; to seek appropriate and creative responses; to ask for explicit and concrete help from others, but without coercing them, since asking is one thing, but demanding is something completely different.

On the one hand, we pay little attention to and rarely talk about our needs—in the context of marriage, family, community life, friendships—and how to satisfy them within the framework of Christian living. Needs do not have to be problematic, nor should they be avoided. On the contrary, it is crucial to consider them and respond to them in alignment with one's personal life choice. On the other hand, we often allow ourselves to become polarized by our unmet needs, making them the center of our existence, even to the point of demanding from others and making claims of rights, among other things. We frequently project the responsibility for our unmet needs onto others. We focus on "what I have not been given that I was due." But maybe we forget that we haven't asked or made explicit what we truly needed, believing that others should guess or thinking that expressing needs is a bad thing. Perhaps, in addition, we have not paid attention to what others needed.

Living our needs

Needs do not have to distance us from God; rather, they are part of the journey to an encounter with God. They speak to us of what genuinely inhabits us and of our existential quests. Allowing ourselves to be discovered, or allowing God to discover us in them, offers us the possibility of a total conversion of our whole being. In addition, if we ask and let God act, he will teach us to respond to our needs in his own way, so different from our own. If we look at the journey of the people of Israel in the desert for forty years, we will discover that it is a paradigm for us to recognize how God knows and meets our needs, even the most basic ones: "You in your great mercies did not forsake them in the wilderness; the pillar of cloud that led them in the way did not leave them by day, nor the pillar of fire by night that gave them light on the way by which they should go. You gave your good spirit to instruct them, and did not withhold your manna from their mouths, and gave them water for their thirst. Forty years you sustained them in the wilderness so that they lacked nothing; their clothes did not wear out and their feet did not swell" (Neh 9:19–21; cf. Deut 2:7).

God cared for the people so that they would "understand that one does not live by bread alone, but by every word that comes from the mouth of the LORD" (Deut 8:3). We are called to do the same. The example of the younger son in the parable is also revealing. He left home to seek happiness on his own and only came to his senses when he experienced his hunger and his need (see Luke 15:14–17).

By following the trail of our needs and reflecting on them, we will be led to seek what we truly lack before God, who always welcomes us in our poverty. This is what we ask every time we pray the Our Father: "Give us this day our daily bread" (Matt 6:11). We must not forget that our Father knows what we need before we ask him (cf. Matt 6:8). He knows our deep thirst; it is we who often deny and evade it, like the Samaritan woman at the edge of the well (see John 4). He cares for us in our needs (cf. Matt 6:31–34), so we are to live them in the embrace of God who helps us to take good care of ourselves.

It is important to expose our needs to God so that we can perceive how he suggests we meet them. This does not exempt us of our responsibility, but it does open us with confidence to seek answers his way. Sometimes, it will seem that God is leading us to what we would expect; at other times, it will seem that he is leading us astray, asking us to wait, or even leaving us empty-handed. This is also part of his pedagogy. It is necessary to experience God stripping us bare so as to fill us, without this meaning negligence on his part (cf. Phil 2:5–9).

We tend to cling too tightly to what we need. We must learn to let go and do without satisfaction when it is necessary. The process of responding to our needs, based on the gospel and on love, often includes renouncing what our needs demand, if it is better for us and for others, giving our lives for the kingdom (cf. Luke 9:23–25). Like Paul, who learned to live at God's pace, we will be able to say: "Not that I am referring to being in need; for I have learned to be content with whatever I have. I know what it is to have little, and I know what it is to have plenty. In any and all circumstances I have learned the secret of being well-fed and of going hungry, of having plenty and of being in need. I can do all things through him who strengthens me" (Phil 4:11–13).

Consequently, we will learn to be free from our needs out of love for ourselves, God, and others, without sterile frustration: "Only by giving up being selfishly occupied with one's needs does a person become open to accommodate God's plan."[9]

All of this requires proper discernment, because the right relationship with our needs will lead us to live detachment with joy. A sober life is liberating and capable of greater enjoyment, because it experiences the value of each thing—of each person—and learns to enjoy the simplest things, as different, austere, and thoughtful ways can be sought to satisfy our needs.

Welcoming the needs of others

Healthy attention to our own needs leads us, inevitably and with the same radicality, to welcome, pay attention to, and perceive and respond to the needs of others, especially those of the people we love and who love us. It is in this dimension that relationships develop and grow in reciprocity or, on the contrary, become impoverished and empty to the point of losing their meaning. The quality of our relationships depends on our mutual capacity to empathize and respond to our own and others' needs, not creating unhealthy dependencies but liberating interdependencies. Christian love challenges us in the face of others: "We know love by this, that he laid down his life for us—and we ought to lay down our lives for one another. How does God's love abide in anyone who has the world's goods and sees a brother or sister in need and yet refuses help. Little children, let us love, not in word or speech, but in truth and action" (1 John 3:16–18).

Love is concrete, not imaginary. Not only do our neighbors have physical needs, but, like us, they also lack many other things. Nor are the goods we possess merely material. The maturity of gospel living undoubtedly involves responding with empathetic responsibility and discerning commitment to the needs that others present to us, without closing our hearts, using the many resources that we have and can share.

Deepening our understanding of the needs of Jesus

It is remarkable that Jesus became aware of his own needs: for water (see John 4:7), food (see Matt 4:2; 21:18), rest (see John 4:6; Mark 6:31), security (see John 7:1), welcome (see Luke 7:44–46), friendship (see John 12:1–2), solitude (see Matt 14:23), autonomy (see Luke 2:46–49), gratitude (see Luke 17:17), affection (see Mark 14:6–9), and others.

Jesus was able to notice and respond to the needs of others because he knew his own needs and responded to them. He did not repress his needs, but he also did not remain closed in their selfish satisfaction. He made the needs of others the priority of his life, living as a servant (see Luke 22:27). He continually went out to meet the needs of those around him, sometimes because they asked him to (see Matt 15:22; Mark 10:47–48; Luke 23:42), and other times because he took the initiative himself, as in the multiplication of the loaves (see Matt 15:32), with the paralytic at the pool (see John 5:6), at the death of the only son of the widowed mother (see Luke 11:7–14), with the man with the withered hand (see Mark 3:1–5), and with so many others.

Jesus recognized and lived with a sense of need. According to the Gospel of John, he died with a cry of need on his lips: "I am thirsty" (John 19:28). He was thirsty. This thirst reflects the radical need of all human beings. We thirst for one another and ultimately for God.

Allowing Ourselves to Be Loved in Order to Love

We are moving into the most central space of our lives and our relationship with God. It is essential that we allow God's love to dwell in us. We need to open our affectivity to the action of grace.

If it is difficult to become aware of what we feel and need, it is even harder to recognize how our affectivity impacts and controls us, because it is well hidden within us. Affectivity is the realm that grants us our greatest identity, where we experience our strength and beauty, but also where we discover ourselves to be most vulnerable and fragile. This vulnerability leads us to protect and defend ourselves, even to the point of attacking and reacting to any imminent threat. It is the most personal and intimate place where we do not let just anyone in. In the face of our affectivity, we are very selective and cautiously distrustful.

To explore a healthy and spiritual experience of our affectivity we need to:

- view human affection positively
- discover our own needs and sources of affection
- acknowledge our own self-rejection
- confront our affective obsessions
- learn to pray affectively
- allow ourselves to be emptied by God

These are the key points of this section. At the end, we will also consider how Jesus lived affectively.

Viewing human affection positively

First, let's consider the importance of viewing human affection in a positive light. God's love has often been presented as incompatible with other affective relationships, in the name of a misplaced holiness. Unfortunately, in the context of religious life, the love of God is often seen in direct opposition to human relationships, affirming the goodness of the former and the supposed evil of the latter. This has led at times to a disdain for the goodness of human love, an undervaluing of friendship, an anomalous distance between people who claim to follow Jesus in a more radical way, a repression of feelings, and a crippled experience of affectivity. No proposal for Christian living can overlook the fact that human relationships are the most beautiful, the most evangelical, and the most important aspect of life. In fact, at the heart of Christianity lies love given and received in deep and naturally human relationships. Affection is so highly valued in the Bible that it becomes a symbol, a mirror, and an analogy of God's own love for his people and for each person. In this passage, as in many others, we can see the strength of filial relationships: "You shall nurse and be carried on her arm, and dandled on her knees. As a mother comforts her child, so I will comfort you; you shall be comforted in Jerusalem" (Isa 66:12–13; cf. Luke 15:11–32). The Bible speaks beautifully of the marriage relationship between man and woman as a reflection of divine love: "For as a young man marries a young woman, so shall your builder marry you, and as the bridegroom rejoices over the bride, so shall your God rejoice over you" (Isa 62:5). The whole book of Song of Songs is also a mirror of this (see Song 1—8).

Friendships are treated in the Bible in a sublime way. The Book of Sirach presents the friend as a treasure (see Sir 6:14–17). Friendship is the fulfillment of the second commandment of the Law: "You shall love your neighbor as yourself" (Lev 19:18; cf. Matt 22:39). Jesus assures us: "No one has greater love than this, to lay down one's life for one's friends" (John 15:13).

God asks us not to have other gods apart from him, but he doesn't say we can't have other loves in our lives (cf. Exod 20:3–5). Living fully means growing in shared love. Discovering and developing our affectivity entails learning to love and be loved in the everyday, natural and necessary, human relationships we have.

Moreover, paraphrasing St. John in his Letters, we cannot love God and allow ourselves to be loved by him whom we do not see if we do not love and allow ourselves to be loved by people of flesh and blood whom we do see (see 1 John 4:20). In Christianity, the love received and given to God is concretely and unambiguously translated into the love shared among us (cf. Matt 25:31–46). The affection of human relationships is God teaching for us; it is a human bond; it is a divine leading-string, and it is a link to the trinitarian communion (cf. Hos 11:4).

In this context, we must also affirm that it is very difficult for us to allow ourselves to be loved. It is much more arduous than trying to love, even though it may not seem that way.

When we love, we are the protagonists, we earn merits, we think we are in control of the situation, we harvest gratitude, we can feel superior and good because we are doing something proper and necessary (cf. Matt 6:2–3). But when we allow ourselves to be loved, we lose control of the situation, we become vulnerable, we are receivers and debtors of what is given to us, and we may even feel inferior. But we will only love if we allow ourselves to be loved first. We will only be unconditional in our love if we experience being loved unconditionally (cf. Luke 7:47; John 13:8; 1 John 4:19).

Similarly, we need to learn to love ourselves well, with all our fragility and greatness. We often become our own worst enemies when we need to be our own best friends. We need to learn to treat ourselves with the same affection and firmness with which God takes care of us. The second commandment is to love our neighbor as ourselves (see Luke 10:27–28). Only by loving ourselves well will we learn to love others well.

Discovering our own needs and sources of affection

Knowing our affective world requires discovering our needs and sources of affection. With this understanding in mind, let us look at the dialogue between Jesus and the Samaritan woman as a roadmap: "'Go, call your husband, and come back.' The woman answered him, 'I have no husband.' Jesus said to her, 'You are right in saying, "I have no husband"; for you have had five husbands, and the one you have now is not your husband. What you have said is true!'" (John 4:16–18).

If we interpret this text from the perspective of affectivity, we can translate Jesus's request as "Go and call on the one from whom you seek to quench your thirst for love." The woman replies that she has no husband, although she is trying to drink affectively from the present companion, who is not her husband. Jesus remarks that she has already had five husbands, six if we count the present one, and yet she is still thirsty, dry, and alone, without a source of affection capable of satisfying her. Thus, by asking her for something to drink, the Master becomes a mirror of her thirst, because he wants to give her living water: an affectivity fulfilled by God that becomes a spring (see John 4:7, 10, 14).

This is the dialogue that Jesus longs to have with each one of us in our deep thirst, in our wells, in our search for affection. We must open wide our affective intimacy before him so that he can unveil us with his deep acceptance and fill us with his grace.

Like the Samaritan woman, we need to formulate our real affective needs,[10] our wells and the sources from which we try to satisfy them. We must beg not to succumb to the fear of being thirsty, not to give in to the shame of our thirst, not to shy away from the asceticism of standing at noon without a bucket beside our deep well, not to evade the constant effort of seeking and telling the truth so as not to be deceived. Only in this way will we be able to recognize with sincerity what determines us affectively.

Affections provide us with a sense of purpose when they are well-lived, but if they are disintegrated, they can abuse, distract, imprison, and even destroy us. It is necessary to ask God for his grace to transform us to know the affections that need to be integrated and liberated, without always being denied or viewed with suspicion. He never abandons us and always comes to meet us in truth, acceptance, and mercy. God knows the clay that forms us. God teaches us to love and to let ourselves be loved.

Acknowledging our own self-rejection

Amid all this, we cannot forget the paradox of self-rejection that we mentioned in the previous chapter,[11] because it marks, above all, and in an indelible way, the experience of affectivity. Our imperious need to be loved and our inestimable divine worth are always confronted with the contradictory resistance of letting ourselves be loved for who we simply and truly are, with the consequent temptation of not being able to accept and acknowledge gratuitous love without doing something to deserve it. On the one hand, we need love like the air to breathe, but on the other hand, we deny it, undervalue it, shun it, suffocating inwardly as we despise ourselves.

This inner belief that tells us that we are not worthy of being loved largely determines our needs and our search for affection. Because we experience and believe that we are unloved or even unlovable, we feel empty, and nothing seems to quench our thirst. By remaining hostage to this lie, we prevent anything or anyone, even God, from dissuading and filling us. Love may surround us, but if we believe that we are unlovable and unworthy, it will slip away and fail to reach us. We will try to win it and trap it again and again, but it will not fill us. We will enjoy it for a time, but soon the emotional experiences of inadequacy, pride, or unworthiness will become stronger, pushing us toward the need for more love and affection, turning the search into a vicious circle. As happened to the Samaritan woman, no husband—after we have had so many—will suffice or fill us, and the well will remain deep (see John 4:11, 16–18).

Therefore, it is essential to recognize how this false belief betrays us affectively in the first-person singular. To ask for the grace to recognize the trickery of the *false self* that constantly makes us want to win the love of others in artificial ways so as not to be left alone, and that tries to convince everyone, by its own strength and talents, that it is worthy of love. The *false self* feeds on fear. It lives on constant and persuasive attempts to convince others that it is worthy. It thrives on self-justification and conquest. Consequently, it always lives outward, pretending to be what it believes it should be in front of God, of itself, and of others. It tries by every conceivable and socially acceptable means to gain approval, prestige, or pleasure.

The only way to become free—in love and to love—is by courageously confronting in God's presence the affective lies that inhabit us and constantly demand ever more proofs and spaces of love to fill our threatened affective identity.

Self-rejection can only be overcome through the living experience of the certainty—offered to us by God and those who love us well—that we are worthy simply for being who we are and not for what we do, have, or achieve, or for what others say about us. To do this, we need to place ourselves under the truth of love that leads us to the truth: "You are loved no matter what."

This gentle, true, and kind voice speaks to us in various forms and tones: through our parents, friends, and teachers, those who love us, and even numerous strangers who cross our path. There are many people who treat us with affection, authenticity, and reverence, reflecting our beauty. They teach us the truth of love and encourage us to keep going even when we are about to give up. We must ask to believe these experiences that proclaim our truth, beyond the inner lie that drags us down. We must make room for the words and gestures, both from those who love us and from God, to convince us that we are lovable and loved.

Facing our affective obsessions

A disintegrated affectivity, determined by the influence of self-rejection, tends to become a destructive force in people's lives, like a river running out of control. Its predatory and self-centered impulsiveness needs to be exposed, overcome, and redirected so that affection can be lived with true love and freedom. Only by knowing the dynamics of affectivity can we truly master it without repression and without blocks or lies that force us to look for disguised and dangerous shortcuts that wear us down.

In our affective quest, we can become obsessed with someone or something as if it were the total and eternal answer to our affection. We can turn that person, thing, or activity into an idol, a vice, a god, losing freedom, maturity, and the ability to love with spiritual detachment. We experience moments or periods of total infatuation, believing that this person or reality will be the answer to all our illusions. Deep down, we think that without it our life will have no meaning; it will be empty.

Similarly, power, possessions, and pleasure function as great temptations, compensations, and affective pursuits. We seek them because we believe that through them we can attain the experience of being loved, valued, and needed; of being useful, protagonists, important; of being taken into account; of having a good time, relaxing, or avoiding pain and suffering, among many other affective rewards. But in the end, they are nothing more than mirages that empty us out in the short term, deceive us, and spoil our affectivity if they are poorly lived or taken as affective ends in themselves (cf. John 4:13; 10:10).

We must also examine and discern whether the love, dedication, and service we try to give to others is truly free and selfless. Often our seemingly loving gestures may conceal attempts to control and manipulate others or implicit quests for human approval and glory to feed our affectivity (cf. Matt 23:5; John 5:44).

Regardless, in all these situations, we need to stand before ourselves and God in spirit and in truth, like the Samaritan woman (cf. John 4:24). It is essential to know the inner movements that shape us, the affective needs that demand attention, and the way we try to respond to them, even when it is difficult to accept them because they betray or embarrass us.

Distancing ourselves from ourselves or from God is futile, for all he desires is to help us experience love as a liberating force that will, in turn, liberate others. Whether married or celibate, parents with their children or children with their parents, friends with one another, all of us—as relational beings—need to enter this dynamic of purification and profound freedom so as not to possess other people by wanting them to constantly and totally respond to our personal affective needs. This is impossible and frightening, but unfortunately all too common.

No human relationship can ever fully satisfy us, no matter how legitimate, beautiful, and necessary it may be. If we try to turn others into a response to our demanding affectivity, we will end up manipulating them or ourselves in some way. In human existence, there is a space of unavoidable loneliness. We must embrace human love as an obligatory bridge in the existential journey, but we must go beyond it to embrace the inherent solitude as an inalienable space for freedom and growth.

If this is true of people, it is even more so of things. There is nothing, no reality, no activity, that can fully satisfy our affective needs. Everything that presents itself to us as a total and Promethean answer is a temptation, a trap, a compensation, and a mirage. We can have everything, do everything; be highly respected, famous, and powerful; walk on paths of heroism; perform exploits and win titles, but our heart will always feel empty and will always ask for more. The heart is made to the measure of God, who "is love," and it is only in him that we should seek the love, received and shared, that satisfies. St. Paul reminds us that even if we had all the gifts and abilities, even if we performed the most incredible deeds, without love we would be useless and nothing (see 1 Cor 13:1–3).

Learning to pray affectively

Freedom means reorienting our affectivity to be able to freely choose and want what God desires for us. For this reason, our affectivity needs prayer.

Living without seeking human reward at every step means losing oneself in God: when you pray, when you fast, when you give alms, when you do good, do it in secret and enter the hidden place of your heart, and God, who is and sees you in that secret place, will reward you (cf. Matt 6:1–18). Reward is an affective experience that is received, and only God holds the key to our deepest affectivity.

Opening our affectivity to God means allowing him to love us, to tell us who we are, to touch our affective resistances, our lack of freedom, our wounds, our fear of not being loved, and to conquer our tendency not to live from him. By his hand, we will learn to overcome the lie of self-rejection. And this can only be done with much prayerful silence, with much trust, with much listening to the Word of God, with much waiting, with much sacramental grace, with the certain hope that he will not fail "because God's love has been poured into our hearts through the Holy Spirit that has been given to us" (Rom 5:5).

To pray affectively is to place ourselves before God, to be aware of our needs, to ask him to reveal our deep thirst and to give us the living water we desire so that we do not have to make an effort to drink from wells of stagnant water that make us even thirstier. Our well is not only deep but often empty. To reach its bottom is not easy. It requires both a life-long journey of spiritual integration, both prayerful and psycho-emotional, through which God fulfills us (cf. John 4:11–15; 6:35; 7:37–38).

Prayer takes time and practice to go through the inner spaces we have seen—sensations, thoughts, feelings, and needs—until we make room for our affective space. Sometimes in prayer, we want to go straight to the experience of God's love without going through all this. God is God and can give it to us, but usually he respects our human rhythms and wants to walk through our inner steps. The deep and continuous reconstruction of our affectivity is possible if we allow God to enter those mysterious and seldom-traveled passages of our inner world. True conversion occurs only when God touches our affectivity and disturbs it; when he embraces, conquers, transforms, liberates, and strengthens us from within, to the point of making us capable of letting ourselves be loved and love like Jesus.

His word, which is truth (cf. John 17:17), wants to resonate over our affective reality: "I have called you by name...I am yours as you are mine" (Isa 43:1); "I have taken you in my hands and covered you with the shadow of my embrace" (Isa 49:2); "I look upon you with infinite tenderness and care for you with more care, even, than a mother cares for her child" (Ps 27:10); "I formed you in the depths of the earth and in your mother's womb" (Ps 139:13); "You are my beloved child, with you I am well pleased" (Matt 3:17); "Nothing can ever separate you from my love manifested in Christ" (Rom 8:38–39).

Finally, entering our affective space before God requires contemplative prayer, which falls in adoration and silence before his presence, with all that we are. The healing we seek is not our own merit or the result of our own efforts but rather of what happens to us in prayer, when we spend long periods in contemplative silence before God, allowing him to touch the depths of our being and from there transform us by his grace. Contemplation is a game of gazes before his presence, where we gaze at him intently, knowing that he is looking at us. And it is his gaze that purifies us, enlightens us, converts us, gives us a new light on reality, communicates his compassion for all, and floods us with a greater knowledge of the life of Jesus Christ. His silent grace shapes our affectivity as we open ourselves to abandoned trust, beyond what we can imagine, until we become living instruments of his love in the service of others.

Allowing ourselves to be emptied by God

To satisfy our affectivity, God almost always chooses disturbing ways of emptying us. He knows that it is very easy for us to seek him for what he gives us, for the miracles we want to see, for the multiplied loaves (cf. John 6:26–27), but not for himself and for who he is. He knows that we easily make him our size, to fill our ego and our affectivity, and therefore he often strips us bare.

This experience of emptiness, of night, of meaninglessness is essential because it helps us to purify not only our relationship with God but also our relationship with ourselves and with others. Only in this way will we move from a false perception based on ourselves to a more real image based solely on who God is, even if this means a painful break with the past and an unsettling openness to the future.

John of the Cross is one of the greatest witnesses to this reality. He was an excellent connoisseur of the human heart with and without God—in its great self-deceptions, its enslavements, its evasions, its tendencies, its clinging attachments, and its subterfuges. This holy man made us partakers of his great gift by leaving us clues to know God's paths at human crossroads.

John shows us how God desires to take us by the hand through the "night," through the "nothingness," through the cross, to the "living flame of love," to the resurrection, to the configuration with Christ, and to the fullest possible communion on this earth with the Triune God. The path he proposes to us is arduous, difficult, and impossible, unless we allow ourselves to be guided by the Spirit, the only one who knows how to lead us with "wisdom and gentleness," respecting the pace of each one of us according to our true capacity for love. Until, like Paul, we can say and live that what we once considered gain, we now consider loss before the supreme advantage of knowing Christ Jesus (see Phil 3:7–9).

Discovering the affectivity of Jesus

Turning our attention to the affectivity of Jesus, we can affirm that he positively lived human affectivity (cf. Matt 11:18; Luke 15:1). He recognized his own affective needs as well as the sources from where to fulfill them (cf. Matt 16:21–23; John 12:27). He did not allow himself to be fooled by the deceptive, though tempting, promises of love (cf. John 6:15). He related to the Father with affection (cf. Matt 3:17; John 12:28; 15:9) and allowed himself to be emptied until he was filled in an unsuspected way (cf. Matt 27:46; Luke 24:25).

Many of Jesus's encounters in the Gospels are affective. In them, Jesus engages the affective needs of each person. He tries to touch the value of the person in their intimacy, to restore their dignity before God, before others, and before themselves. Through his words and gestures, Jesus wants each person to discover who he or she is for God. Jesus expresses the mercy and compassion of the Father. He has a special commitment to those who are marginalized by the law, restoring them to citizenship in the kingdom. This can be seen, for example, in the way he relates to the paralytic lowered from the roof by his friends. Before healing him, Jesus forgives his sins and restores him affectively: "Son, your sins are forgiven" (Mark 2:5). He first affirms his identity as a son so as to heal him of his paralysis. The great paralysis we all suffer is not recognizing our true selves and not living in the certainty that, no matter what happens, we are sons and daughters.

In the gospel, there are also many women who testify to having a dignified and worthy place in the eyes of Jesus, even though they held little value in that society. The scene of the woman who approaches and touches him secretly and in a forbidden way, as she was considered impure, is very suggestive. Once again, Jesus insists on the relationship by asking who has touched him. When the woman, full of courage—because she knows that she has done something she should not have—confesses what has happened, she hears, instead of a condemnation, a recitation of her value in the words of the Master: "Daughter, your faith has made you well; go in peace, and be healed of your disease" (Mark 5:34). Again, the affective affirmation of divine filiation is at the center of Jesus's intention, translated into words and gestures.

Similarly, if we turn to the anointing at Bethany, we discover how Jesus allowed himself to be loved and cared for by that woman, praising her action. She "came with an alabaster jar of very costly ointment of nard, and she broke open the jar and poured the ointment on his head" (Mark 14:3). In the face of indignant criticism, Jesus acknowledges and accepts her gesture of affectionate kindness: "Let her alone; why do you trouble her? She has performed a good service for me" (Mark 14:6).

Jesus loved not only the poor but also the rich. We can see this, for example, in the scene with the man who was looking for something more. Faced with his restlessness, Jesus engaged him in an affectionate dialogue: he looked at him steadily and loved him. Only then did he call him to follow him, asking him to leave everything (see Mark 10:21).

Friendship is an essential part of Jesus's life. It is his affective constitution. We see this in his visits to the house of Lazarus, Martha, and Mary, among other scenes, as the Gospels tell us: "Accordingly, though Jesus loved Martha and her sister and Lazarus" (John 11:5). It is astonishing that the gospel narrative refers to these characters in this way, reflecting what was in the affective space inhabited by the four. Jesus considered them friends and fostered his relationship with them, from the coordinates of God (see Luke 10:38–42), allowing himself to be cared for by them (see John 12:1–8). Friendship is the summary and culmination of Jesus's relationship with his disciples. At the end of his life, before the Passion, he says to them: "I do not call you servants any longer, because the servant does not know what the master is doing; but I have called you friends, because I have made known to you everything that I have heard from my Father" (John 15:15).

The character who narrates the life of Jesus in the fourth Gospel describes himself as "the disciple whom Jesus loved" (John 21:20; cf. John 13:23; 19:26; 20:2; 21:7, 24). What an unusual way to describe oneself. To recapitulate what discipleship is, the author of John's Gospel does not reveal his name, most certainly so that each one of us may discover ourselves in that same identity, as we follow him: "You are the one whom Jesus loves."

Another deeply affective space is offered to us by the word "bridegroom": "Jesus said to them, 'The wedding guests cannot fast while the bridegroom is with them, can they? As long as they have the bridegroom with them, they cannot fast'" (Mark 2:19). In the fourth Gospel, John the Baptist presents Jesus as the bridegroom: "He who has the bride is the bridegroom. The friend of the bridegroom, who stands and hears him, rejoices greatly at the bridegroom's voice. For this reason my joy has been fulfilled" (John 3:29). Jesus is the bridegroom, while his disciples are the bridegroom's friends. Who is the bride? We are both the friends of the bridegroom—we accompany him, we want to announce him, we want to make him known—and also the bride, the one who shares the love of the bridegroom in mutual affection. We are therefore invited to this deep friendship and nuptial relationship with Jesus, as the prophet proclaimed: "And I will take you for my wife forever;

I will take you for my wife in righteousness and in justice, in steadfast love, and in mercy" (Hos 2:19).

In Jesus, we see that he let himself be loved and loved deeply because he let himself be loved and loved the Father, whom he called Abba, deeply (see Mark 14:36). In Jesus, the experience of the Father's love was so central and strong (cf. Mark 9:7; John 10:17; 17:24–26) that it enabled him to love to the incomprehensible extreme of the cross. There, by freely and lovingly laying down his life for us, he transformed what was torture and evil into a compassionate surrender on our behalf. In the face of this terrible contradiction, he revealed the extreme of God's love, which knows no end (cf. John 13:1; 1 Cor 13:8). Such is the omnipotence of love that is capable of this miracle.

Jesus wants to introduce us into his own relationship with the Father, into that "God so loved the world" (cf. John 3:16; 17:22–23; Rom 8:15), so that we may always live as sons and daughters. He urges us, now and always, to perpetuate the chain of his love in the time of the world through our affectionate relationship with him: "I give you a new commandment, that you love one another. Just as I have loved you, you also should love one another. By this everyone will know that you are my disciples, if you have love for one another" (John 13:34–35).

Learning to Desire

Learning from Jesus's desire

To learn how to desire, we need to look to Jesus in his relationship with desires.

At the beginning of the Last Supper, Jesus said: "I have *eagerly desired* to eat this Passover with you before I suffer; for I tell you, I will not eat it until it is fulfilled in the kingdom of God" (Luke 22:15–16).

The two Greek words used, the noun *epidsumía* (desire) and the verb *epidsuméo* (to desire), express a very strong longing, and moreover, the two terms reinforce each other: with desire I have desired. The second word is the same one used by Jesus when he speaks of a man's sensual desire for a woman, committing the sin of adultery in his heart (see Matt 5:28), and when, in the parable, he speaks of the younger son's desire to eat the swine's food because he was hungry (see Luke 15:16).

The expressions used in Luke's passage denote an intense and polarizing desire on the part of Jesus. At the Last Supper, it is an expression of his intense desire to share the Passover with his apostles. Desire floods his entire being, his whole body and his whole person—it is not something superficial or skin deep. It is the meaning of his life, his passion, and his death. He deeply desires to love them, to give himself up, to be received in his gift, to celebrate the kingdom, and to lead them into the presence of God. Jesus does not withhold his desire; he welcomes it, he feels it, he expresses it, and he translates it into action. The Master does not hide or despise his desires. Jesus desired. Desire shaped his life.

In the Gospels, another word that expresses desire is *dsélo*: "I came to bring fire to the earth, and how I wish it were already kindled!" (Luke 12:49). It appears frequently in the New Testament, sometimes with the meaning of "desire" and other times as "wanting something" and "fulfillment."

There are many scenes where we can find *dsélo* expressing a sense of desire. In the famous golden rule: "In everything do to others as you would have them do to you; for this is the law and the prophets" (Matt 7:12). In the earnest plea of the Canaanite mother for Jesus to heal her daughter after he had refused. Jesus, at the woman's insistence, agreed and said, "'Woman, great is your faith! Let it be done for you as you wish.' And her daughter was healed instantly" (Matt 15:28). In the request of another mother, that of the Zebedee sons: "And he said to her, 'What do you want?' She said to him, 'Declare that these two sons of mine will sit, one at your right hand and one at your left, in your kingdom.' But Jesus answered, 'You do not know what you are asking'" (Matt 20:21–22). Jesus did not reject desire but rather embraced it as something natural. He encouraged people to treat others according to their wishes, he listened to the wishes of others and let them change his own attitude, and he did not reject them even when they expressed something inappropriate, such as the request to sit at his right hand and at his left.

The man from Nazareth was also an heir to the biblical tradition of his people. If we read through the Old Testament, we see that the landscape of Scripture is full of desires. The biblical man lives desire naturally and often with a great emotional charge: "my soul thirsts for you; my flesh faints for you" (Ps 63:1); "My soul longs, indeed it faints for the courts of the Lord" (Ps 84:2). Moreover, the God who reveals himself in the Bible listens to human desire: "O Lord, you will hear the desire of the meek; you will strengthen their heart, you will incline your ear" (Ps 10:17).

Therefore, Jesus does not hide his desires and, in turn, has a peculiar way of awakening, engaging, and bringing to light the desires of those he encounters. His first words in the Gospel of John, addressed to John's disciples who followed him, are: "What are you looking for?" (John 1:38); with this question he asks them to formulate the desires that motivate them to follow him. At the end of the same Gospel, he addresses similar words, now in the singular, to Mary Magdalene: "Jesus said to her, 'Woman, why are you weeping? Whom are you looking for?'" (John 20:15), prompting her to express the desire that tormented her: to find the Master's dead body.

In the Sermon on the Mount, Jesus said: "Blessed are those who hunger and thirst for righteousness, for they will be filled" (Matt 5:6). Jesus links our basic needs of hunger and thirst, which are survival instincts and powerful experiences of longing, to the deep yearning for justice. At the Feast of Tents, where the Jewish people celebrated the passage through the desert by remembering the thirst for water and God's providence, Jesus appeals to desires: "On the last day of the festival, the great day, while Jesus was standing there, he cried out, 'Let anyone who is thirsty come to me, and let the one who believes in me drink. As the scripture has said, "Out of the believer's heart shall flow rivers of living water."' Now he said this about the Spirit, which believers in him were to receive; for as yet there was no Spirit, because Jesus was not yet glorified" (John 7:37–39). Jesus was also thirsty, an expression not only of need but also of profound desire; he deeply wanted us to recognize our thirst for him and to desire his Spirit (cf. John 4:7; 19:28).

Discerning the desires

These gospel texts, among many others, show us that the relationship with Jesus and the reception of his word lead us to discover our desires to unfold them before his. It is therefore necessary to enter the cellar where our longings dwell so as to include them in our prayer. We may have very beautiful ideas about God and following him, but what secretly helps us in our decision is what we feel and desire as the treasure and lord of our lives (cf. Luke 12:34; 16:13). We are only God's when his grace penetrates us deeply, touches us, fulfills us, and heals our affectivity, embracing and loosening the tangle of our desires, encouraging us to desire to run toward what lies ahead (cf. Phil 3:7–14).

In his presence and sustained by his grace, we can and must delve into our desires. We do not need to be afraid or persistently distance ourselves from them, as we are sometimes led to believe, thinking that they will lead us astray from the path of the Spirit. But neither should we forget that we can become slaves to our desires, making us dependent on things, activities, and even people, leaving no free space for God. There are too many addictive attachments, even to small things, that hurt and numb us, robbing us of what is essential and hijacking our lives: the compulsion to mobile phones, social media, games, shopping, food, entertainment, alcohol, or other vices, resulting in the inability to be alone, still, and focused.

For this reason, learning to desire involves discerning our desires, asking God until we desire according to the Spirit and not according to what harms us (cf. Gal 5:16–17; Rom 8:5–6). Discernment helps us to identify our desires and the way we relate to them. Some questions can help us: Do we desire, or do we believe that we should not desire? Do we pay attention to our desires? Do we listen to them, or, on the contrary, do we try to ignore them in a titanic struggle? Do we believe that our desires must always be fulfilled? Do our desires drive our lives? Do we express our desires, or do we keep them locked away in that inner corner where there is a door with a sign saying "No Trespassing"? Do we place our desires before God in a prayerful space? Do we ask God to teach us to desire and to increase our desire for the good?

In the first chapter, we said that desire encompasses a constellation of inner movements. Placing ourselves before God with our desires involves recognizing those internal motions that lead to the elaboration of desiring so as to perceive what motivates us, where it comes from, and where it wants to take us.

Our desires mirror our unmet needs—both the most complex and the most basic—but they become obstacles if we remain on the surface, confusing them and being determined by the imperative impulse of the moment, without discerning what and how best to respond to them. The desires that truly give meaning to life are those that aim beyond their satisfaction because they are directed toward transcendence: we should not desire merely to love but to be transformed into love by Love itself.

Seeking and allowing God to transform our desires involves understanding how we relate to our needs, especially our affectivity; how we seek and desire to see them fulfilled; how we embrace and accept the dissatisfaction of inevitable limitations; how we endure and integrate frustration for a greater good; and how we explore God's ways that are often very different from our own.

All this requires prayer, accompaniment, and discernment because of its inherent complexity and subtlety. Knowing ourselves so as to decipher ourselves with purity of heart (cf. Matt 5:8), even in the movements of desire that lead us beyond ourselves, is an apprenticeship of freedom.

Desiring well

When our desires lead us in the right direction, we should be able to enjoy them and follow the Spirit's footsteps in them. But if they lead us in a direction that is contrary to God, we need to ask for the grace to recognize what is happening, to be transformed from within and set free to desire what he desires. Perhaps the power of the affective desire of our self-rejection is betraying and making us long for that which does not satisfy or fulfill us. Its influence will lead us, paradoxically, to seek and be content with too little, with small pleasures, incapable of satisfying our thirst for the infinite. Only God can satisfy us with his gratuitous gift. Therefore, educating our desires is learning to open our eyes to what really satiates us, freeing us from what are very small pleasures. We need to learn to desire more and better without getting caught up in what is salt water that does not quench our thirst. Moreover, it is not about ceasing to desire but rather about often renouncing the immediacy and tyranny of desire.

St. Augustine teaches us to desire while waiting for God's time, who in his fullness makes us wait so as to increase our interior space. By delaying the gift, desire grows, and God increases our capacity to receive a greater gift.

To desire in a deeper way also means to go through the well-known Ignatian indifference. This is not the absence of desire but rather learning to desire while being free regarding what is desired. St. Ignatius himself tells us in the First Principle and Foundation[12] that we are to use created things insofar as they help us, so we are to become indifferent, to distance ourselves from them if they harm us, to desire and choose only that which leads us to the goal for which we were created. It is not a question of eliminating desire but of learning, purifying, and strengthening it in the direction that builds us up. It is about awakening and deepening the desire for God.

A well-lived desire is vital, for it gives color, brightness, and attractive beauty to the professed value that, without it, would remain in the realm of obligation, rigidity, and imposition. In life, lasting achievement and changes will only come about if there is a genuine desire for transformation and growth that withstands the setbacks that always arise. In the often unforeseen and costly difficulties, desire is tested or refined, or it disappears, depending on its foundation and strength.

We cannot live in a constant struggle between desire and reason, nor between desire and will. This would not last long and would do a lot of damage. When desire overrides the will, a person lives according to his whims and without any restraint. If one, however, tries to eliminate desires from the inner life, the person would fall into the rigidity of voluntarism, fulfillment, and moralism, losing the ability to savor and enjoy life. In this way, the person loses the possibility of living with joy, gratuitousness, and generosity; living, rather, in fear of and compliance with the law and role, of efficiency, and according to what others will say. He or she will not live from beauty, or from gratuitousness, or from friendship abundantly received, shared, and desired. The person will cling to the legalism that Jesus so criticized: "Woe to you, scribes and Pharisees, hypocrites! For you tithe mint, dill, and cummin, and have neglected the weightier matters of the law: justice and mercy and faith. It is these you ought to have practiced without neglecting the others" (Matt 23:23). And how many people are there in the church who have unlearned desire?

We conclude this section on the need to learn to desire with an inevitable question: How do we attend to the desires of others? Being aware of our own desires enables us and inevitably requires us to be attentive to the desires of others, not to rush out and satisfy all their longings but to be able to appreciate them with empathy, to become aware of them, and thus, together, find suitable ways that lead us to the authentic sources that satisfy us (cf. Ps 87:7).

Wanting What God Wants

Saying: "Your will be done"

What we ask God for in each Our Father is: "Your will be done, on earth as it is in heaven" (Matt 6:10). That means wanting to do what God wants! We need to know not only God's will but also our own, and ask that his will be done, not the other way around.

Wanting to know God's will requires discovering the real, affective and effective weight that his will represents for us: Do I believe that his will can be known? Do I believe that what God wants is the best for me and for others? Am I afraid of his will? Do I trust that he will give me the strength to do his will? How and where does God reveal his will in our daily lives? And so many other questions that arise on the path of life, when we place ourselves before his designs that are so different from our own.

The answer to these questions will also allow us to recognize the many resistances we have—because of our upbringing, personality, experience, and self-rejection, as well as the social environments in which we are immersed—that often push us away from God's will. At the same time, there is already much of God's will that we desire that shows itself in our behaviors and attitudes.

Likewise, we cannot assume that we are doing God's will simply because we ask for it and say it in our prayers. It is very easy to express that we are seeking his will when, in fact, we are deviating from the path. Insightful discernment will help us because God's will is neither easy to understand nor easy to carry out, since we think with human measures and not divine ones (cf. Matt 16:23). It is even more difficult if we unconsciously want to carry out our own will at all costs, both in small and large deliberations. Although we make very great sacrifices and choices that seem very holy, it may be that they do not seek or embody God's will, and, therefore, they are of no use to us because we are building on sand, even becoming, according to Jesus, agents of iniquity (see Matt 7:21–27).

This is where self-rejection, camouflaged in a false and disordered love of self, plays tricks on us. Without realizing it, we may want to use God's will in our favor to feed our ego, our prestige, and our fame. We may seem to be saying and even wanting to do his will, but deep down we are driven by our lack of freedom and our affective deceptions. We may even pursue good things, projects, and perhaps brilliant ideas, while not really seeking the love of God but rather self-justification and the ability to impose our own will on situations and others.

Self-deception is very subtle and very common in the spiritual life. Therefore, we need to learn to have both a clear and gentle will in the face of life's events, since each person can understand and grasp different nuances of God's will in the same situation. Only dialogue, attentive listening, and common discernment can lead us to understand the totality of his will, without clinging to our own as the only expression of the divine will.

To follow Jesus is to follow his ways and not the ways we would rather choose and claim. To follow him requires a voluntary willingness to love always, even if it means falling into the earth, sacrificing oneself, losing everything, even one's own will, to gain him alone (cf. John 12:23–26; Phil 3:8). To follow Jesus is to want, like him, to embrace the Passover of the Father's will (cf. Matt 26:39). To follow him is to desire to let go of our will, realizing that others and life can also be an expression of God's will beyond our understanding.

Following Jesus requires prayerful, sincere, and obedient listening. In prayer, as we have seen, we allow God to meet us in the sensations we experience, to inform our thoughts, to provide what we need, to touch us in our affectivity by showing us his love, and to embrace our desires by transforming them. In the same way, God purifies and strengthens our will to conform it to his, if we ask him to do so. For this, we need to place ourselves freely and willingly in his hands, with acts of faith and pure trust. It is not enough to understand what is good to live it; we must ask for the strength to will it and to live it, "for it is God who is at work in you, enabling you both to will and to work for his good pleasure" (Phil 2:13).

In prayer, we need to give a lot of space to discover our will and God's will, to confront them both, and to let God lead us in our willingness to accept his and to let go of ours. This takes time and much loving grace in a filial relationship. It requires openness and availability—real freedom—to accept God's plans. Freedom is wanting and committing to do what God wants.

Contemplative prayer is fundamentally about lovingly consenting to God's will. This implies opening our inner spaces before God and silently kneeling our will before him, asking that his will, known or hidden, desired or resisted, possible or impossible for us, be done in us, with our consent and by his grace (cf. Luke 22:42). Without our consent, God will not force us, but with our "yes," he can do what we dare not even ask or imagine, because it does not fit into our human mind and transcends our possibilities (cf. 1 Cor 2:9; Eph 3:20). We need to remain silent before him for long periods of time, asking him to consent to his will in our lives.

Wanting what God wants will lead us to the goal of our life that is union with him. Union with God is not just an emotional experience of pleasant moments but also a uniting our will with his, our love with his, allowing him to love in us. Union with God is to allow ourselves to be drawn into the trinitarian dance of communion of life and wills that transforms us from within into love poured out for many.

Wanting as Jesus wanted

By his life, Jesus teaches us practically and tangibly not to hesitate to place ourselves in the hands of the Father, and to surrender our will to him. This does not mean, however, that we renounce our own will, extinguishing it or ignoring it, but rather the opposite. There are several encounters of Jesus in which the will of the interlocutors is at the center of the scene. A leper appeals to Jesus's will, at the beginning of his public life, to heal him: "If you choose, you can make me clean" (Mark 1:40). Jesus responds by expressing his will: "I do choose. Be made clean!" (Mark 1:41).

In other circumstances, it is Jesus who asks. "Then Jesus said to him, 'What do you want me to do for you?' The blind man said to him, 'My teacher, let me see again.' Jesus said to him, 'Go; your faith has made you well.' Immediately he regained his sight and followed him on the way" (Mark 10:51–52). In this case, Jesus does not assume what the blind man wants but inquires about his will. And only when the answer is confirmed does he heal him. It seems that Jesus needs the blind man to explicitly state his will to be healed so that he can do what he wants.

In the same way, Jesus asks us: What do you want me to do for you? He wants and needs us to state explicitly what we really want in our relationship with him. For it may be that, like the sons of Zebedee, we do not want to see but rather to sit with prestige and power at his right and left, or like the indignant disciples, we want to fight for the first places (see Mark 10:36–41).

Jesus, heir to the Jewish tradition, knew that God's will meant happiness for his people. That is why he did and said nothing on his own but sought in everything not his own will but the will of the Father who sent him (see John 5:30; 12:49). His adherence to the Father's will was total, to the point of considering it his food (see John 4:34), trusting it even in the most painful and absurd moments, as in Gethsemane (see Matt 26:42), and of being "obedient to the point of death—even death on a cross" (Phil 2:8), learning obedience through suffering (see Heb 5:8).

Jesus embodied the prayer of the psalmist: "Sacrifice and offering you do not desire, but you have given me an open ear. Burnt offering and sin offering you have not required. Then I said, 'Here I am; in the scroll of the book it is written of me. I delight to do your will, O my God; your law is within my heart'" (Ps 40:7–9; cf. Heb 10:5–10).

Jesus sanctified us by always living in accordance with the Father, even to the point of freely giving himself up on the cross out of love, so that God's will could be fulfilled in us: our sanctification (see 1 Thess 4:3). Through his resurrection, he makes it possible for our will to be united with his every step of the way, so that we may always want, gently, firmly, and freely, what God wants.

Deciding in Freedom

Deciding freely and responsibly

We are constantly making decisions. The journey of life is paved with the countless decisions that shape our day-to-day existence. Both big and small decisions chart our existential path. Therefore, it is essential that we be able to make decisions freely, in coherence with the proposal of the gospel and with our fundamental life choice. This means deciding according to what is good for us and for others from God's perspective; with knowledge of what is happening around us; being free from what prevents us from following Jesus on the way (cf. Mark 10:21–22); so as to come to love as he did (cf. John 13:34–35).

Often, many people make important life decisions without being aware of what they are doing, without adequately preparing or considering the consequences, letting themselves be carried away by momentary impulses, external pressures, or the opinions of others.

However, many are also aware of the delicate consequences that their choices will have, both for themselves and for others, and prefer to opt for well-founded and considered decisions. The aim of what has been proposed up to now is for us to go through our inner selves so that, more aware of the movements that inhabit us and freed from our attachments, we can reach the threshold of decisions with greater responsible freedom. Thus, the act of deciding becomes an exercise of personal authenticity and coherence of life, because it is the result of a personal choice and not of blind instincts or subjection to external realities, sometimes unknown but overwhelming.

Making good decisions involves being aware of our motivations, the decisions we want to make or have made, and the consequences that this has caused or will cause in ourselves and others. It is also necessary to allow life itself to confirm, readjust, or challenge the decisions made. All our decisions must be part of our relationship with God, both those we have already made in the past and those we are making or have yet to make in the future.

Even if we have made mistakes in our decisions and the consequences may be serious, we must affirm with total conviction that we can always start again. We need to try as hard as we can to reach the right decisions, but one or more bad or wrong decisions, our own or those of others, can never mean the end of the path if we open ourselves to God, as so many have done throughout history, because his grace is stronger than our weakness and sin (cf. Rom 8:37–39; 2 Cor 12:8). Among them, we can think of Peter, who after denying Jesus allowed himself to be reached by his merciful gaze that recovered him (see Luke 22:54–61). We can also think of Paul, who allowed himself to be forged by God's compassion, reconciling his personal history, and making him an apostle to the Gentiles (see 1 Tim 1:12–14). The Easter proclamation reminds us that it is always possible to start again, even after the fall, abandonment, abuse, error, death, and denial. God can make all things new (cf. Rev 21:5). If we return and allow him, he transforms us even with our sin (cf. Luke 7:47).

At every crossroad in life, we need to place ourselves under God's merciful grace so that he can renew us and continue to show us the way to go. If we have made mistakes, he will help us to ask for forgiveness and to forgive, to reconcile ourselves with our own history and with others, to get up and correct our course.

Consider the "what" and the "how"

In decision-making, we cannot simply stay at the level of what to do: Should I do this or that? Is this path or that one better? Is it convenient to do this or not? Do I say yes or no? This step, inherent in decision-making, is essential but not complete. When deciding what to do, we must also consider how to do it. The "how" is as important as the "what" because it affects the consequences of what is done and radically changes the impact of the responses on ourselves and others. We must dedicate time and thought to how the decision will be carried out. For example, I may decide to talk to a person, but I also need to consider and decide the inner attitude with which I will approach them, the tone of voice, the content of the conversation, the words I will use, the place, the time, and so on. All these details are essential and require reflection when making such a decision.

When considering the various possible decisions—their pros and cons—and which decision we should make, it is necessary to ask God for light to develop realistic, possible, and appropriate response strategies to the situations in question. At the same time, we must implore the gift of creativity so that the decisions we make can also be new, bold, focused from new perspectives, and not always conventional. Creativity makes us participate in God's action, which invites us to be co-creators with him of our own lives, the lives of others, history, and the world with the imprint of the kingdom. With God, we can seek and offer new, courageous, and updated responses to the original problems of today, avoiding the temptation to give the same comfortable answers of yesterday, and without clinging to the criterion of "we have always done it this way" (*Evangelii Gaudium*, 33). In addition, new challenges require, even more, new and bold responses, for "one puts new wine into fresh wineskins" (Mark 2:22).

To decide well, effectively, and creatively, we need time to place the situations and the search for a response in the prayerful space that we open before God, so that we can be guided by him. It is essential to be helped by people who, as experts in the way of following Jesus, can warn and guide us, but never decide for us.

Choosing Jesus

Jesus chose and invited us to choose freely, accepting decisions without forcing anyone, because true love liberates. His whole life was full of small and big decisions, pondered and discerned, that in the end led him to embrace the cross, not by chance but by a voluntary and decisive surrender on our behalf.

Jesus spent time in prayer to discern well the decisions he had to make. He was guided by what he understood from the Father, by the fundamental direction of his life, and not by what circumstances he was in or what others might seem to impose at any given moment: "In the morning, while it was still very dark, he got up and went out to a deserted place, and there he prayed. And Simon and his companions hunted for him. When they found him, they said to him, 'Everyone is searching for you.' He answered, 'Let us go on to the neighboring towns, so that I may proclaim the message there also; for that is what I came out to do'" (Mark 1:35–38; cf. John 11:4–6, 14).

In relation to cultural and religious conditioning, Jesus was not a rebel who simply opposed the religious institution. The Gospels show him to be obedient to his parents (see Luke 2:51), to the Jewish customs, times, and feasts (see Matt 21:17–18; Luke 4:16; John 5:1; 7:10). However, he also decided not to give in to what was unjust and hypocritical in religious practice. For this reason, he clashed with the Pharisees and with everything that was unfair (see Matthew 23). He did what was not allowed on the Sabbath (see Mark 2:24), going against one of the strongest Jewish rules of his time, knowing that it would cost him his life (see Mark 2:23—3:6). Jesus chose to live by God's mercy and not by sacrifice (see Matt 12:7). He was obedient to the Jewish law, but he also surpassed it (see Matt 5:17). He was aware of the consequences of his decisions: in his speeches (see Luke 4:23–30; John 6:60), parables (see Luke 20:9–20), miracles (see John 5:16), and gestures (see Mark 11:15–18), and in the way he welcomed those who approached him in search of his company and the true face of God (see Luke 15).

Jesus was free, both from religious and political authorities, free from others without being determined by anyone (see Mark 12:14), free from temptations (see Matt 4:1–11) and from sin (see John 8:46), and free from events that he welcomed without forcing them and through which he carried out his mission with unwavering determination. Jesus was also free to choose before God. He obeys him not out of fear or obligation but because he is the beloved Son who chooses to love the Father in everything (see John 14:31).

At the end of his life, although Jesus knew that he was frowned upon by the religious powers, he decided not to give up, even if he had to encounter death. His freedom was total, both in external and internal realities. He was free from ties to love always and from the extreme: "When the days drew near for him to be taken up, he set his face to go to Jerusalem" (Luke 9:51); "The Father loves me, because I lay down my life in order to take it up again. No one takes it from me, but I lay it down of my own accord" (John 10:17–18); "Now my soul is troubled. And what should I say—'Father, save me from this hour'? No, it is for this reason that I have come to this hour. Father, glorify your name" (John 12:27–28); "the world may know that I love the Father. Rise, let us be on our way" (John 14:31).

His decision "to lay down one's life for one's friends" (John 15:13) was not sudden but voluntary, thought out, prepared and confirmed by the words and gestures of his last hours: in the institution of the Eucharist (see Luke 22:19–20); in the gesture of washing the feet of his disciples (see John 13:1, 3–5); and in the pardon he asked for on behalf of those who would kill him (see Luke 23:34).

The Gospels are full of decisions that help us to appreciate how Jesus appeals to our human capacity for decision-making, so that we may always follow him, without him ever manipulating us. Jesus invites us to decide before him with clarity, definition, and determination: "Then he said to them all, 'If any want to become my followers, let them deny themselves and take up their cross daily and follow me...'" (Luke 9:23); "Jesus said to him, 'No one who puts a hand to the plow and looks back is fit for the kingdom of God'" (Luke 9:62); "Because of this many of his disciples turned back and no longer went about with him. So Jesus asked the twelve, 'Do you also wish to go away?' Simon Peter answered him, 'Lord, to whom can we go? You have the words of eternal life. We have come to believe and know that you are the Holy One of God'" (John 6:66–69). At every step, Jesus wants to give us the grace to make the free decision to follow and choose him.

Following Jesus Along the Way

Taking action

"Not everyone who says to me, 'Lord, Lord,' will enter the kingdom of heaven, but only the one who does the will of my Father in heaven" (Matt 7:21). From the perspective of discipleship, action is essential. The decision is called to be translated into action. It cannot remain forever in the realm of good ideas. Action is the embodiment of the decision taken, it gives it substance, concreteness, and realism. Our concrete actions—which also include our omissions—are like a gauge that allows us to know whether our relationship with God is true, whether in practice we allow grace to grow stronger in our weakness. It is through our visible fruits that our authenticity is tested: "You will know them by their fruits. Are grapes gathered from thorns, or figs from thistles? In the same way, every good tree bears good fruit, but the bad tree bears bad fruit. A good tree cannot bear bad fruit, nor can a bad tree bear good fruit" (Matt 7:16–18).

This does not mean that everything will be solved at once. We know very well that we need to accept our shortcomings and achievements, starting over again and again, visiting the inner corners of our being with him, to let his grace conquer them through love. Only then will he liberate us from within, until our works give glory to God, even in our fragile clay (cf. Matt 5:16; 2 Cor 4:7).

Moving into action will subject our inner world to new entropies and movements, requiring us to remain attentive to all that continues to affect us so that we can proceed consciously at the pace of life that challenges and shakes us. Our interiority is not separated from our actions but flows into them and is revealed by them. Our actions reveal our inner world because they are rooted in it and are a consequence of it.

In turn, our concrete acts shape our interiority. Only by placing our actions—right or wrong—before the gaze and word of Jesus, without leaving anything out, will we come to know ourselves, live everything in his company, and discern continuously. Amid action, God remains our companion. We cannot relegate him only to the space of quiet and silent moments of prayer. It is amid the hustle and bustle of life, in our Galilee with its challenges, where God accompanies us with his presence and his loving power (cf. Matt 28:10, 16, 20).

Follow him, remain in him, and make disciples

Jesus was always a consistent man, both in his words and gestures, who knew how to translate the experience of God's love into concrete actions. Today, as always, he invites us to do the same: "For I have set you an example, that you also should do as I have done to you" (John 13:15). He sums it up with a powerful word that is both an invitation and an imperative desire. It is the same word that he addressed to his disciples: "Follow me" (Matt 9:9; John 21:22). Following him is the action we are called to live in response to all his outpouring and self-giving, but we can only do this if we remain in his love (cf. John 15:5, 8). The word that he has sown in our interiority, increasingly freed from the hardness of the road, the stones and the thorns, is called to bear fruit through our perseverance and commitment (cf. Luke 8:15; Matt 10:27; Luke 24:48; John 15:16). The entire journey we have undertaken points to being disciples of Jesus, bearing much fruit for the glory of the Father. The goal is to embody the word that is Jesus in such a way that what we have received by his Spirit is translated into his own love: "We love because he first loved us" (1 John 4:19). This is the dynamism of God's gift, which transforms us into himself, making us his voice and his gesture for the good of all. Our action is a grateful response to everything he has done in our land (cf. Isa 55:10–11; Ps 126:3).

But there is more. "We cannot keep from speaking about what we have seen and heard" (Acts 4:20; cf. 1 John 1:3–4). To communicate to others the Good News that we have heard, experienced, and lived is the culmination of the Christian life and, therefore, of any authentic spiritual journey. We cannot remain closed in on ourselves, but God's dynamism opens us up to others and to the world. To act in accordance with the gospel is to pass on to others what we have received from him as free salvation, unearned treasure, and living water that transforms us. From baptism, every Christian is a missionary: all the baptized are "missionary disciples" (*Evangelii Gaudium*, 120).

To be sent and to proclaim Jesus is the fullness of Christian life, because we want to follow Jesus in the way he shows us. The desire and need for others to share in what God has given us is a normal and urgent consequence of having experienced his ineffable love in our clay. Our evangelizing action will enable many to come closer to God, as many others have done with us. We must not forget what St. Paul tells us: "But how are they to call on one in whom they have not believed? And how are they to believe in one of whom they have never heard? And how are they to hear without someone to proclaim him? And how are they to proclaim him unless they are sent?... So faith comes from what is heard, and what is heard comes through the word of Christ" (Rom 10:14–15a, 17).

We are coming to the end of our existential journey through our interiority, and that now moves to external action, only so that we can return to explore our inner spaces again, impacted and impressed by the reality that surrounds us. Thus, in uninterrupted movement, step by step, God becomes the soil of our life, the sea of our beach, the air we breathe, the bread of our thanksgiving, and the water of our well from which we drink and to which we bring others to drink, making a shared experience of the kingdom of God.

The Goal of Freedom

The gift of freedom that Jesus offers us out of love is the goal we aspire to reach. To conclude this third chapter, I will use his own words from the fourth Gospel: "If you continue in my word, you are truly my disciples; and you will know the truth, and the truth will make you free.... So if the Son makes you free, you will be free indeed" (John 8:31–32, 36).

"If You Make My Word Your Home"

To make his word our home or *to remain in his word* is the first proposition or condition that Jesus sets forth for us to receive his own freedom. To *make his word our home* or *to remain in* (*méno* in Greek) is a verb phrase with a profound meaning in Johannine theology. It means to stay, to abide, to dwell.... In some places it is used to express the mutual immanence between Jesus and the disciple who believes in him. This passage expresses the intimate relationship that believers must have with Jesus, with his word and his message. *To make the word our home*, or *to remain in the word*, means to listen and be faithful to what Jesus has said.

Helping to *remain* has been one of our aspirations at each step of the journey. We have outlined *how* to open our inmost being to his word, to his presence, in a way that is both affectionate and effective, and *how* to allow him to enter into us with his liberating strength, leading us into communion with him. We have indicated clues *to make* his gospel and his love *our home*, accepting and welcoming his *abiding* in us (cf. John 15:3, 5, 7, 9).

"You Will Indeed Be My Disciples"

Welcoming Jesus into our inner world, believing in his love, makes us his *disciples*. In the end, we can say that we have proposed paths of discipleship (cf. John 10:14; 1 John 4:16): adhering to the Master in all aspects of life with radical trust; listening to him and remaining in his message; deciphering the echoes that his word and everyday life provoke within us; allowing ourselves to be transformed by him in concrete ways;

following him in his paths of service and gratuitousness, thus giving glory to the Father and bearing abundant fruit (cf. John 15:1–8).

We have not proposed a spiritual asceticism that is alien to the person of Jesus. The effort to know ourselves in God is only possible and meaningful if it brings us closer to Jesus and to our relationship with him, allowing him to know us, to love us, and to make us his witnesses: disciples ready to accompany him in his steps, even to the cross that leads to the resurrection and to the welcoming of the Spirit. We have opened ourselves to his word so that we can dwell in the intratrinitarian relationship and thus become his disciples (cf. John 14:16–23).

In addition, we have sought to follow in the footsteps of the "disciple whom Jesus loved" (cf. John 13:23; 19:26; 20:2; 21:7, 20). To be loved in John's Gospel is to believe, and to believe is to allow oneself to be loved. Just as Jesus believed and experienced the boundless love of the Father, the disciple is called to believe by allowing him- or herself to be loved unconditionally to the end (cf. John 13:1, 8; 15:9; 1 John 4:16) and to bear witness to this so that others may believe by letting themselves be loved (cf. John 1:14; 19:35; 20:31).

"You Will Come to Know the Truth"

In the biblical context, *to know* has a profound meaning: it goes beyond human knowledge and expresses a knowledge through experience, the fruit of an intimate existential relationship. In some contexts, it means the sexual intercourse between a man and a woman (see Gen 4:1; Matt 1:25). We only *know* a person or a thing if we have concrete experience of it. *To know* God is to experience and be introduced into his intimacy. In the Gospel of John, *knowing* also means communion (see John 1:3), participation in the divine life itself (see

14:17–24), and perfect union in true love (see 17:26). One of the dynamics that inspired these pages was that of *knowing*: to experience, to enter our interiority, to accept God's invitation to share intimacy, and to allow ourselves to be led to the *truth*.

Truth, in the Gospel of John, is an omnipresent and deeply meaningful concept. *Truth* is dynamic; it renews itself and always renews those who accept it, giving them light and fullness. It is not a theoretical or static *truth* but Jesus himself: the Father's word of *truth* given as a gift to humanity. Moreover, the *truth* that is Jesus makes human beings his brothers and sisters, as they become children who remain forever in the Father's house (see John 8:35; 14:6). We have tried to *know* God in spirit and in *truth* (cf. John 4:24).

We have also outlined proposals for how to open our authentic thirst and to drink from his living water that he offers us. Like the Samaritan woman, we have allowed ourselves to be questioned in our lives with sincerity, without hiding anything, so that he could offer us the *truth* that transforms us (cf. John 4:16–18).

Our sincere search for *truth* in Jesus has accompanied us, for it is the only way we can travel to reach the Father (cf. John 14:6). Knowing Jesus and knowing ourselves in him is essential, so that, like the Samaritan woman, we may have the saving experience that he gives to our ambiguous humanity, wounded by our circumstances and deep, stagnant wells that do not satisfy us (cf. John 4:28–29).

"And the Truth Will Set You Free"

We have presented paths to inner *freedom*, so that the truth may transform and *liberate* us. Jesus's invitation has moved us to be able to attain *freedom*, which is the gift he offers to those who enter into a relationship with him, by giving them his own life.

The *freedom* to live according to who we truly are and what we were created for is what we wanted to present as a task, gift, and fruit. *Free* people are those who, by the power of grace, continue to choose God. They are *free* because they do not have to earn demanding merits that enslave them, nor do they claim prestige or usurp it at the cost of self-justifying fulfillments that lead to fear. They are *free* because they do not use others or allow themselves to be used by the ambition of success. They are *free* because they live in the liberating truth and in the true freedom of knowing that they are the beloved son or daughter, the Father's delight, and because they trust in God's gratuitous abundance. They are *free*, not for lack of commitment but to commit themselves entirely to the point of living the dynamism of the wheat grain that dies to bear fruit (cf. John 12:24). They are *free* to be able to say at every step: "Your will be done" (Matt 6:10b). They are *free* because the Son makes them free—they are not slaves.

Freedom has consequences, especially in our relationship with others and with the world, since it leads us to follow in the footsteps of Jesus toward his greatest testimony of love (cf. John 15:13–14). Authentic Christian love forgets itself; it is a total gift because it participates in the absolute gift of God and translates it. This is to love truly.

A free life embraces its own nakedness before oneself, before God, and before others, without doubting the love that surrounds us. A free life, inundated by the Holy Spirit, finds and creates the free space to pour itself out completely from its own smallness.

Allowing ourselves to be loved and to love is to set out on a journey toward the goal of freedom, since the *liberation* that Christ offers us is fulfilled in "faith working through love" (Gal 5:6). God liberates us from ourselves and from the slavery of sin so as to make us "servants of one another in love" (Gal

5:13; cf. Rom 6:17–18, 22). This is the goal to be reached: *freedom in the filial love* that Jesus gives us.

"If the Son Sets You Free, You Will Indeed Be Free"

Jesus himself confirms this: "Very truly, I tell you, everyone who commits sin is a slave to sin. The slave does not have a permanent place in the household; the son has a place there forever. So if the Son makes you free, you will be free indeed" (John 8:34–36).

That is why we are *so fragile and so loved*, because the Son introduces us into his own relationship with the Father who sets us free. Throughout this whole journey, Jesus has been our way, our truth, and our life (cf. John 14:6). He has blessed us with all kinds of gifts so that we may become sons and daughters of God (cf. Eph 1:3–5) and live as such. The same love that he received in the trinitarian relationship is given to us through his incarnation, passion, death, and resurrection. His Spirit, as Son, is poured out into our hearts and gives us the trinitarian love that sets us free from everything that alienates us from God (cf. Rom 5:5; Eph 2:13). With steadfast hope, we know that we will reach the goal of freedom, for the Son sets us free. We are free because he has loved us, because he has visited and embraced every corner of our human condition, because his love is stronger in us than our resistances to love, because he makes himself the way and accompanies us on the journey to freedom, because his love conquers our capacity to love, and because he lives and loves in us.

Conclusion

So Fragile and So Loved

Looking Back at the Journey

"You cannot plumb the depths of the human heart or understand the workings of the human mind; how do you expect to search out God, who made all these things, and find out his mind or comprehend his thought? No, my brothers, do not anger the Lord our God" (Jdt 8:14). This striking verse from the Book of Judith echoes what we have proposed throughout this exposition, through which we have pursued different objectives. We have drawn a cartography to understand the incomprehensible human heart in the common experiences of everyday life. We have proposed bridges of integration between the different personal places without underestimating the complex human fragility. We have asked questions to awaken our conscience, so often frightened and confused by the many contradictory and involuntary inner movements. We have offered words of reconciliation; we have discovered unknown inner places inhabited by the divine. We have suggested ways of approaching and knowing God, who comes to us to conquer our freedom through love. We have opened spaces to allow ourselves to be led by the Holy Spirit, who recreates us in divine filiation. We have learned to trust more in grace. We have shown the way into the potter's house to allow God to inspire our clay.

God took on our humanity in Jesus and saved us. Yet it is we who often block our acceptance of his salvation. We have therefore sought to identify some of the obstacles that prevent us from radically embracing his incarnation in our human flesh so as to discover and overcome them with the power of grace. Using the image of the resurrection of Lazarus, we have removed the stone because we heard the loud voice of Jesus: "Come out." We have helped to unbind the bandages that imprison us in our destructive fears so that we can receive the salvation that restores new life into us for the glory of God (cf. John 11:39–44).

Consequently, we have embarked on a journey toward freedom, proposing guidelines that allow God to transform us into the image of his Son (cf. Rom 8:29): as fragile and as loved as Jesus, we are called increasingly to abandon the slavery of everything that prevents us from being nourished by his will and carrying out his work (cf. John 4:34).

One of the central realities that we have observed is that our temperament determines the way we relate to God and the way we pray. Each person is original, and this characterizes their relationship with themselves, with others, with the world in general, and also with God. Self-knowledge helps each person to discover their original way of welcoming God, his revelation, and his way of living Christian spirituality. Some people are more sensitive to the body, others more rational, others more emotional, and so on. Taking this into account allows for a better integration of the whole person, without believing that there is a one-size-fits-all spirituality. Knowing oneself in God facilitates the acceptance of different ways of approaching God, seeking personal ways of prayer, welcoming the differences of others, and living what is authentically Christian—building bridges instead of insurmountable walls.

Our proposal for inner knowledge does not mean self-absorption. Although we have offered a personal process, we do not at any time accept that this leads us to self-centeredness or to forget about others. What we propose is just the opposite: to pay attention to our inner self and to allow God to enter all aspects of existence is not a feat motivated by selfishness; it is, above all, an essential exercise that allows us to decipher and embrace our fragility. It strengthens us to stand strong before the loving mystery of God, enables us to discern his will, teaches us to go out ourselves, challenges us to welcome others in their diversity, and leads us to embrace our mission in the world with more authenticity.

In the context of following Jesus, there are many people who believe that paying attention to one's inner self is a waste of time and a lack of Christian radicality. The person who tries to respond to Jesus's call goes through his or her own experience of having nowhere to lay one's head and of not closing oneself off to self-interest. However, that can never mean ignorance, unawareness of oneself and of what one lives inside. Detachment from self to be able to love necessarily claims knowledge of self, being aware of one's personal experiences, allowing oneself to be loved by the love that reaches out to us, and thus loving others sincerely, freely, and unselfishly. How many psychological, spiritual, and social problems arise from the unconsciousness and negligence of what is happening within us?

Moreover, being aware of what we live is essential to being witnesses of the gospel. The true content of what we have to offer as Good News arises from the deep experience of love and freedom. The mission of communicating to others cannot be based on what we only know by hearsay (cf. Job 42:5) but on what we have seen, heard, and touched firsthand (cf. 1 John 1:1–4). Others perceive whether what we proclaim is true in us or not. We are called to be not only teachers but authentic witnesses who believe in what they preach, live what they believe, and truly preach what they live. In the end, we do not merely transmit what we say, but who we deeply are, pray, and live.

Learning to let God visit our innermost selves has, therefore, many practical consequences for all aspects of life that are worth exploring further. Living God within us will change our relationship not only with ourselves but with our entire environment. Our relationships with our family, our marriage, our friendships, our work, our community, and all that the world presents to us will never be the same when lived from the deep freedom of being loved in our fragile clay. How many of our relationships suffer from our inability to love and receive love? How many of our relationships are enslaved by our enslavements? Discovering that we are loved to the depths of our being and freed from what keeps us focused on ourselves will allow our relationships to change, grow, and mature. It will also allow us to be catalysts for the freedom of others.

For example, let us look at the importance of personal and mutual knowledge in couple relationships for building sincere and fruitful life dialogues, beyond the self-rejection that becomes an armor of defense and attack. The greater the intimacy, the greater the fear of not being worthy of being loved for who I am. Misunderstandings often stem from fear and the lack of acceptance of what it means to be human, with all our frailties and challenges. If both spouses explore God's unconditional love together, they will learn to disarm themselves before each other. This will help them to create a stronger and more resilient relationship, which will be more genuine because both will be more real and true to each other.

Another relationship that changes radically when we live our true divine filiation is the one we have with the world. Ecology is an intrinsic reality of the Christian faith: "Creation itself will be set free from its enslavement to decay and will obtain the freedom of the glory of the children of God" (Rom 8:21). A proper experience of our inner self will lead us to an authentic integral ecology, both human, natural, and cosmic. The paths we propose have real repercussions for how we care for our common planet and live justice in solidarity. Those who live at peace with themselves and others enjoy a more sober, joyful, happier, and more fulfilled lifestyle, without the obsession of consumption—a less devastating approach for the planet and others (*Laudato Si'*, 222–27). Respect and care for the cosmos and the fair distribution of goods require us to be sons and daughters of God, freed by the Spirit of love to desire what is good and not what destroys (cf. Rom 8:5–6).

Friendship as Journey and Goal

The journey toward the fullness of God necessarily and without detours takes place through the human experience, by way of the intricate web of relationships, of love shared and offered, rejected and learned, denied and accepted, through the tangle of human bonds and knots. That is why we conclude by speaking of friendship, because when it is true, it becomes the fullness of love. Friendship is both the journey and the goal of the human experience.

In the Book of Sirach, we read: "Faithful friends are a sturdy shelter; whoever finds one has found a treasure. Faithful friends are beyond price; no amount can balance their worth. Faithful friends are life-saving medicine, and those who fear the Lord will find them. Those who fear the Lord direct their friendship aright, for as they are, so are their neighbors also" (Sir 6:14–17). Jesus himself, at the end of his life, sums up his relationship with his own by proposing friendship as a road-map: "No one has greater love than this, to lay down one's life for one's friends. You are my friends if you do what I command you. I do not call you servants any longer, because the servant does not know what the master is doing, but I have called you friends, because I have made known to you everything that I have heard from my Father" (John 15:13–15).

Throughout history, and in an extreme way in the Incarnation, God has come to meet us, offering us his own love, made flesh and friendship. But this relationship can only be built and can only grow if there is a response on our part. God waits for and needs our reciprocal response. He can love us without our collaboration, but he cannot complete a friendship with us without our puzzle pieces. He waits for them, leaving us free to place them humbly and gratefully.

Living a life rooted in God and proclaiming his message is only possible, authentic, and credible through a friendship that seeks to translate his love for each human being. The people we love and by whom we are loved become human strings of God. The friend is a sacrament of God. Friendship is a reflection, path, and witness of the trinitarian love. Friendship is a bridge to God; it is a divine experience. There is an urgent need to rediscover the power of authentic and disinterested friendship that becomes a path of encounter, knowledge, and self-discovery. Friendship is an essential place of love and freedom.

The wisdom of St. Francis of Assisi eloquently summarizes the value of friendship and reveals a horizon as unexpected as it is true: "Look, to evangelize a person is to tell someone: 'You too are loved by God in the Lord Jesus.' And not only to say it, but to really think it. And not just to think it, but to behave with that person in such a way that they feel and discover that there is something saved in them, something greater and more noble than they thought, and that they are awakened thus to a new awareness of themselves. That is to announce the Good News to them. We can only do this by offering them our friendship, a true, disinterested friendship, without condescension, made of trust and deep esteem."[1]

A true friend is one who invites us to be ourselves and who, at the same time, helps us to be the best version of ourselves as our identities evolve. Loving our friends involves the great risk of reciprocity, of loving and being loved freely, without trapping or possessing, without submission or exploitation, without domination or manipulation. Loving in the hope of being loved, and loving even when we are not loved, always in profound freedom. And if this is not the case, it is no longer friendship. That is why friendship is the culmination of any full human relationship. All relationships of love are either friendships or have no consistency. Friendships give meaning to life because they bring our totality into play and make us live to the full our very reason for being—to love and to be loved.

Friendship can reach spaces of intimacy that do not have to be genital. Although many times in our society, sexuality, genitality, and intimacy are confused, this is not true. Friendship can be one of selfless and magnanimous intimacy. Only those who truly love us can conquer our true intimacy, to reach our most intimate selves, beyond our skin, our defensive fears and resistant masks. With them, we dare to reveal ourselves, becoming vulnerable and weaving a tapestry of mutual intimacy, respectful proximity, and necessary space. Only those who truly love us can decipher who we are and help us to change through calm acceptance, firm demand, and supportive kindness. Those who truly love us do not settle for our mediocrity; instead, they challenge us to be better, believing in us. Only the people we truly love and befriend matter to us beyond the necessary sacrifices and the price to be paid in the ups and downs of the relationship. Only friendship makes us step out of our walls and comfort zone toward the promised land of shared love that begets freedom. Authentic friendship never remains confined to a closed circle but instead builds open spaces that welcome others.

We cannot expect all of our relationships to follow the path of true friendship, but we cannot live without authentic friendships. They alone allow us to develop our full human and divine potential.

The journey we have proposed culminates in friendship and is only possible through friendship. We can never walk it alone. We need friends, and we need to be friends. We need our beauty to be remembered and reflected in the gaze, words, and gestures of those who love us. We need to remember, to witness, and to reflect the beauty of others. We need to become friends with ourselves, with others, and with God, journeying together in freedom. We need to let ourselves become friends with God: to be fully human, embracing both fragility, freedom, and love.

Afterword

As you have read this book, I trust that you have felt encouraged to embark on the process that Paula invites us to undertake, a process articulated around two keys for the life of every person: love and freedom.

It is not difficult to agree with Paula that we need a pedagogy for freedom embodied in our fragile humanity that, at the same time, can allow itself to be strengthened and liberated by the power of God to live his will in all things.

Three steps have been proposed to us. The first is self-knowledge of the inner world, exploring the diverse aspects and dimensions that are found in every person. This is an inescapable step that has been presented in an original way. The second is the knowledge that God loves us unconditionally, and that we often resist this incontestable truth. In a society driven by effectiveness, we must believe that our salvation lies not in what we do but in what we receive; we must beware of placing the law above grace, rules above mercy, mandates, or commandments, no matter where they come from, above the love we owe to all who, like us, are the image of the same God.

This is how we arrive at Paula's proposal to reach freedom, which is the only thing that makes a full life possible. Now comes the time for the concrete and pedagogical "hows" necessary to reach the goal. The book now immerses us in a kind of symphony, in which this pedagogy appears to us as something we will need our entire lives. Paula does not offer us solutions, simply because there are none, and in this, the proposal you have in your hands is like the book of the Spiritual Exercises of St. Ignatius. Neither book is meant to simply be read; they are proposals that must be experienced. The pedagogy of freedom that is presented to us must be attempted, for only to the extent that we reach this freedom (or a certain degree of it) can we say that we have traveled this path.

This book also draws upon and reflects many of the intuitions of Ignatian spirituality, beginning with the central theme of the book, the search for freedom. It is precisely through the lens of freedom that St. Ignatius contemplates the human being, and at the center of every person, thoughts and desires are the key to discernment, leading to the right choices that point to an action that can only be of service to all. A correlation can also be drawn between the parable of affectivity that the author proposes (an original contribution) and what in the Spiritual Exercises is called the first way of praying: St. Ignatius begins with the senses, for only by using them can we truly change. Only by transforming our sensory way of being in the world can we change the way we use our faculties—memory, thought, and will—ultimately attaining the same attitudes as Christ.

Having come to the end of this book, all that remains for you is to try embarking on the process that has been shown to us, to write your own journey of liberation, in the same way this book is the result of a personal, spiritual, pastoral, and academic journey, a synthesis of inherited ecclesial richness, the wisdom of many authors, of what has been studied and received along the way, the insights from accompanying many people and oneself, the lived experience of prayer, and the ongoing pursuit of the gospel paths, with all its stumbles and triumphs.

Diego Molina, SJ

Appendix

List of Sensations

Open	Ticklish	Cold	Dizzy	Thirsty
Aching	Feverish	Hungry	Nauseous	Smiling
Struck	Distracted	Icy	Nervous	Soft
Tight	Electric	Wounded	Palpitating	Sweaty
Tied	Energized	Tingling	Heavy	Stifled
Hot	Sick	Hollow	Burning	Shivering
Calm	Distraught	Unstable	Radiant	Tense
Warm	Sponged	Restless	Relaxed	Hesitant
Closed	Expanded	Released	Stiff	Empty
Tired	Firm	Slight	Healthy	
Frozen	Fluid	Full	Sensitive	
Congested	Frantic	Weepy	Breathless	

List of Feelings*

Abandonment	Abasement	Absence	Absorbed	Absorption	Abuse
Acceptance	Accompani-ment	Achievement	Admiration	Affection	Affliction
Aggression	Agitation	Agony	Alarm	Alienation	Alteration
Amazed	Ambivalence	Amusement	Anger	Anguish	Animosity
Annoyance	Anxiety	Apathy	Appreciation	Apprehension	Approval
Arrogance	Astonishment	Attachment	Attention	Attraction	Autonomy
Aversion	Benevolence	Betrayal	Bewilderment	Bewitched	Bitterness
Bliss	Boldness	Boredom	Burnt	Calm	Calmness

Continued

Captivation	Care	Censorship	Centeredness	Clarity	Closeness
Cold	Comfort	Commitment	Compassion	Competence	Complacency
Concentration	Concern	Condescension	Confidence	Confusion	Congestion
Consideration	Consolation	Consternation	Contempt	Contentment	Contrariness
Correspondence	Courage	Covetousness	Curiosity	Daze	Dazzlement
Deception	Defeat	Demotivation	Dependence	Depression	Desire
Desolation	Despair	Despondency	Destruction	Devaluation	Devastation
Dignity	Disappointment	Disbelief	Discomfort	Disconformity	Disconnection
Disconsolation	Discontent	Discord	Discouragement	Discredit	Disdain
Disenchantment	Disgust	Disinterest	Disorientation	Dissatisfaction	Distant
Distraction	Distrust	Domination	Doubt	Dread	Dysphoria
Ecstasy	Empathy	Empowerment	Emptiness	Enchantment	Encouragement
Energetic	Engagement	Ennui	Enthusiasm	Envy	Equanimity
Esteem	Euphoria	Exaltation	Exasperation	Excited	Excitement
Exhaustion	Expectance	Exuberant	Failure	Fascinated	Fatigue
Fear	Fervor	Firmness	Flattery	Fortitude	Fragility
Freedom	Frenzy	Friendship	Fright	Frustration	Fullness
Fury	Generosity	Gloomy	Grief	Grievance	Grumpiness
Guilt	Happiness	Harmony	Hatred	Heartburn	Heaviness
Helplessness	Homesickness	Honesty	Honor	Hope	Horror
Hostility	Humiliation	Humility	Impatience	Imperturbability	Impotence
Inability	Incompatibility	Incongruence	Indifference	Indignation	Inferiority
Insecurity	Inspiration	Instability	Insufficiency	Integrity	Interest
Intolerance	Intrepidity	Intrigue	Invasion	Invigorated	Irate
Irritation	Jealousy	Joy	Jubilation	Judgmental	Justice
Kindness	Lack of love	Lack of protection	Laziness	Lethargy	Loneliness
Longing	Lost	Love	Lust	Meanness	Melancholy
Misery	Misfortune	Mortified	Motivation	Necessity	Nervous
Nostalgia	Nostalgic	Obligation	Obnubilation	Omnipotence	Openness

Optimism	Ostentation	Pacification	Pain	Panic	Paralysis
Passion	Patience	Peace	Perplexity	Persecution	Perturbation
Pessimism	Petrified	Phobia	Pity	Pleasure	Prepotency
Pride	Pudor	Radiant	Rage	Rebelliousness	Refreshed
Regret	Rejection	Rejoicing	Rejuvenated	Relaxed	Relief
Reluctance	Remorse	Renewed	Repudiation	Repulsion	Resentment
Reserve	Resignation	Resilience	Resistance	Respect	Restfulness
Restlessness	Restored	Revenge	Revived	Sadness	Safety
Satisfaction	Sensitive	Separation	Serenity	Shame	Shock
Shyness	Sigh	Solidarity	Sorrow	Stimulated	Strangeness
Stress	Stubbornness	Stupor	Submission	Sufficiency	Support
Surprise	Suspicion	Sympathy	Temperance	Temptation	Tenderness
Tense	Terror	Tiredness	Tolerance	Torn	Tranquility
Turbulence	Turmoil	Understanding	Unhappiness	Unity	Unrest
Vacillation	Value	Vertiginous	Vibrant	Vulnerability	Warmth
Withdrawn	Woundedness	Wrath			

* English translation of F. Aguirre, "Lista de 250 emociones y sentimientos" (List of 250 emotions and feelings), https://psicologos.mx/lista-de-emociones-que-podemos-sentir.php (accessed November 19, 2022).

List of Needs

CONNECTION	CLOSENESS	MEANING	PHYSICAL WELL-BEING
Acceptance	Affection	Learning	Shelter
Appreciation	Love	Self-expression	Water
Coherence	Support	Ability	Air
Collaboration	Warmth	Clarity	Food
Compassion	Closeness	Closure	Comfort
Communication	Company	Commemoration	Rest/sleep
Knowing and being known	Community	Understanding	Space
Connection	Physical contact	Awareness	Sexual expression
Trust	Care	Contribution	Intimacy
Consideration	Gentleness	Creativity	Movement/exercise
Cooperation	Interdependence	Growth	Protection/refuge

Continued

CONNECTION

- Empathy
- To understand and be understood
- Stability
- Inclusion
- Belonging
- Shared reality
- Reciprocity
- Respect/self-respect
- Emotional safety
- Seeing and being seen

CLOSENESS

- Intimacy
- Recognition

MEANING

- Discovery
- Mourning
- Effectiveness
- Variety
- Hope
- Stimulus
- Exploration
- Significance
- Participation
- Realization
- Challenge
- Mission

PHYSICAL WELL-BEING

- Safety
- Silence

INTEGRITY

- Authenticity
- Honesty
- Identity
- Presence
- Sincerity
- Solidarity
- Transparency

CELEBRATION

- Joy
- Celebration
- Fun
- Humor

AUTONOMY

- Choice
- Space
- Spontaneity
- Independence
- Freedom
- Respect

PEACE

- Harmony
- Beauty
- Communion
- Balance
- Spirituality
- Equality
- Order
- Pleasure

Notes

Chapter 1

1. Augustine of Hippo, *Tractates on the Gospel of John*, tractate 10, 1, trans. John Gibb, from *Nicene and Post-Nicene Fathers*, first series, vol. 7, ed. Philip Schaff (Buffalo, NY: Christian Literature Publishing Co., 1888). Revised and edited for New Advent by Kevin Knight, http://www.newadvent.org/fathers/1701010.htm.

2. See Teresa of Avila, *The Book of My Life*, trans. Mirabai Starr (Boston: News Seeds, 2007), 13, 15.

3. Ignatius Loyola, *Spiritual Exercises of St. Ignatius of Loyola*, trans. Louis J. Puhl (Chicago: Loyola Press, 1968) , no. 23, http://www.raggionline.com/saggi/scritti/es/ejercicios.pdf (accessed September 15, 2020).

4. Ignatius Loyola, *Spiritual Exercises*, no. 21.

5. There are some authors who differentiate between these two terms, here we take them as synonyms.

6. As explained above, "affectivity" is defined in the text as the need and capacity for love.

7. Some authors use this word as a synonym for "emotion" or "feeling."

8. English translation of *Mafalda*, a cartoon strip by Quino, https://www.pinterest.es/pin/307722587012143970/(accessed December 29, 2023).

9. St. John of the Cross, "Song of the Soul That Rejoices in Knowing God by Faith"; see https://newtheologicalmovement.blogspot.com/2011/03/most-holy-trinity-as-spring-of-water.html (accessed August 8, 2024).

10. Cf. Pope Francis, Apostolic Exhortation *Gaudete et Exsultate*, March 19, 2018, no. 49, https://www.vatican.va/content/francesco/en/apost_exhortations/documents/papa-francesco_esortazione-ap_20180319_gaudete-et-exsultate.html (accessed December 29, 2023).

11. Viktor E. Frankl, *Man's Search for Meaning* (Boston: Beacon Press, 2006), 65–66.

Chapter 2

1. Teresa of Avila, *The Book of My Life*, trans. Mirabai Starr (Boston: News Seeds, 2007), 48.

2. Thérèse of Lisieux, *The Story of a Soul: The Autobiography of Saint Thérèse of Lisieux (the Little Flower)*, trans. John Clarke, OCD, 3rd ed. (Washington, DC: ICS Publications, 1996), 259.

3. St. Augustine of Hippo, *Confessions*, 1,1.5, see https://www.vatican.va/spirit/documents/spirit_20020821_agostino_en.html (accessed on July 24, 2024).

Chapter 3

1. Eloi Leclerc, *The Wisdom of the Poor One of Assisi* (Santa Ana, CA: Hope Publishing House, 1996), 22.

2. Augustine de Hippo, Sermón 169, 13, https://www.augustinus.it/spagnolo/discorsi/discorso_220_testo.htm (accessed November 19, 2022).

3. See Appendix: "List of Sensations."

4. Henri Nouwen, *Spiritual Direction: Wisdom for the Long Walk of Faith* (New York: HarperOne, 2011), 28.

5. Abi Morgan, "The Iron Lady," screenplay, 57, https://stephenfollows.com/resource-docs/scripts/Iron-Lady-screenplay.pdf (accessed November 19, 2022).

6. See Appendix: "List of Feelings."

7. See "Deciding in Freedom," in chapter 3.

8. See Appendix: "List of Needs."

9. Synod of Bishops, Preparatory Document for the Synod on Youth, January 13, 2017, II. 3, https://www.vatican.va/roman_curia/synod/documents/rc_synod_doc_20170113_documento-preparatorio-xv_en.html (accessed November 19, 2022).

10. The list of human needs in the appendix also includes our emotional needs.

11. See "We Resist Letting Ourselves Be Loved" in chapter 2.

12. Cf. Ignatius Loyola, "First Principle and Foundation," in *Spiritual Exercises of St. Ignatius of Loyola*, trans. Louis J. Puhl, SJ (Chicago: Loyola Press, 1968), 12ff. See also http://www.raggionline.com/saggi/scritti/es/ejercicios.pdf, no. 23 (accessed on September 15, 2020).

Conclusion

1. Leclerc, *The Wisdom of the Poor One of Assisi*, 116.

Bibliography

Aguirre, Francisco. "Lista de 250 emociones y sentimientos" [List of 250 emotions and feelings]. https://psicologos.mx/lista-de-emociones-que-podemos-sentir.php. Accessed November 19, 2022.

Augustine of Hippo. *Confessions*, 1, 1.5. https://www.vatican.va/spirit/documents/spirit_20020821_agostino_en.html. Accessed July 24, 2024.

———. *Sermón 169*. https://www.augustinus.it/spagnolo/discorsi/discorso_220_testo.htm. Accessed November 19, 2022.

———. *Tractates on the Gospel of John*. Tractate 10, 1. Translated by John Gibb. From Nicene and Post-Nicene Fathers, First Series, vol. 7. Edited by Philip Schaff. Buffalo, NY: Christian Literature Publishing Co., 1888. Revised and edited for New Advent by Kevin Knight, http://www.newadvent.org/fathers/1701010.htm. Accessed on August 8, 2024.

Francis, Pope. *Evangelii Gaudium*. Apostolic Exhortation, November 24, 2013. https://www.vatican.va/content/francesco/en/apost_exhortations/documents/papa-francesco_esortazione-ap_20131124_evangelii-gaudium.html. Accessed November 19, 2022.

———. *Gaudete et exsultate*. Apostolic Exhortation, March 19, 2018. https://www.vatican.va/content/francesco/en/apost_exhortations/documents/papa-francesco_esortazione-ap_20180319_gaudete-et-exsultate.html. Accessed November 22, 2022.

———. *Laudato Si': On Care for Our Common Home*. Encyclical Letter, May 24, 2015. https://www.vatican.va/content/francesco/en/encyclicals/documents/papa-francesco_20150524_enciclica-laudato-si.html. Accessed November 19, 2022.

Frankl, Viktor E. *Man's Search for Meaning*. Boston: Beacon Press, 2006.

Ignatius Loyola. *Spiritual Exercises of St. Ignatius of Loyola*. Translated by Louis J. Puhl. Chicago: Loyola Press, 1968. See also http://www.raggionline.com/saggi/scritti/es/ejercicios.pdf. Accessed August 8, 2024.

John of the Cross. "Song of the Soul That Rejoices in Knowing God by Faith." https://newtheologicalmovement.blogspot.com/2011/03/most-holy-trinity-as-spring-of-water.html. Accessed August 8, 2024.

Leclerc, Eloi. *The Wisdom of the Poor One of Assisi*. Santa Ana, CA: Hope Publishing House, 1996.

Morgan, Abi. "The Iron Lady." Screenplay. The Weinstein Company, 2011. https://stephenfollows.com/resource-docs/scripts/Iron-Lady-screenplay.pdf. Accessed November 19, 2022.

Nouwen, Henry, with Michael J. Christensen and Rebecca J. Laird. *Spiritual Direction: Wisdom for the Long Walk of Faith*. New York: HarperOne, 2011.

Second Vatican Council. *Gaudium et Spes*. Pastoral Constitution on the Church in the Modern World, December 7, 1965. https://www.vatican.va/archive/hist_councils/ii_vatican_council/documents/vat-ii_const_19651207_gaudium-et-spes_en.html. Accessed November 19, 2022.

Synod of Bishops. "Young People, the Faith and Vocational Discernment." Preparatory Document, January 13, 2017. https://www.vatican.va/roman_curia/synod/documents/rc_synod_doc_20170113_documento-preparatorio-xv_en.html. Accessed November 19, 2022.

Teresa of Avila, *The Book of My Life*. Translated by Mirabai Starr. Boston: News Seeds, 2007.

Thérèse of Lisieux. *The Story of a Soul: The Autobiography of Saint Thérèse of Lisieux (the Little Flower)*. Translated by John Clarke, OCD. 3rd ed. Washington, DC: ICS Publications, 1996.